Modern Fabric

Modern Fabric

Twenty-Five Designers
on Their Inspiration and Craft

Abby Gilchrist & Amelia Poole

———

PRINCETON ARCHITECTURAL PRESS · NEW YORK

Published by
Princeton Architectural Press
202 Warren Street, Hudson, New York 12534
www.papress.com

Editors: Jan Hartman and Sara Stemen
Designers: Paul Wagner, Natalie Snodgrass

Library of Congress Cataloging-in-Publication Data
Names: Gilchrist, Abby, author. | Poole, Amelia, author.
Title: Modern fabric : twenty-five designers on their inspiration and craft /
    Abby Gilchrist, Amelia Poole.
Description: New York : Princeton Architectural Press, 2020. |
    Summary: "The first collection of modern fabric designers and their work—
    a colorful and inspiring selection featuring fresh, bold patterns from
    an international group of today's up-and-coming and established textile stars"
    —Provided by publisher.
Identifiers: LCCN 2020005884 (print) | LCCN 2020005885 (ebook) |
    ISBN 9781616898373 (hardcover) | ISBN 9781616899677 (epub)
Subjects: LCSH: Textile designers—Interviews. | Textile fabrics. | Textile design.
Classification: LCC NK9502 .G55 2020 (print) |
    LCC NK9502 (ebook) | DDC 746.092—dc23
LC record available at https://lccn.loc.gov/2020005884
LC ebook record available at https://lccn.loc.gov/2020005885

Table of Contents

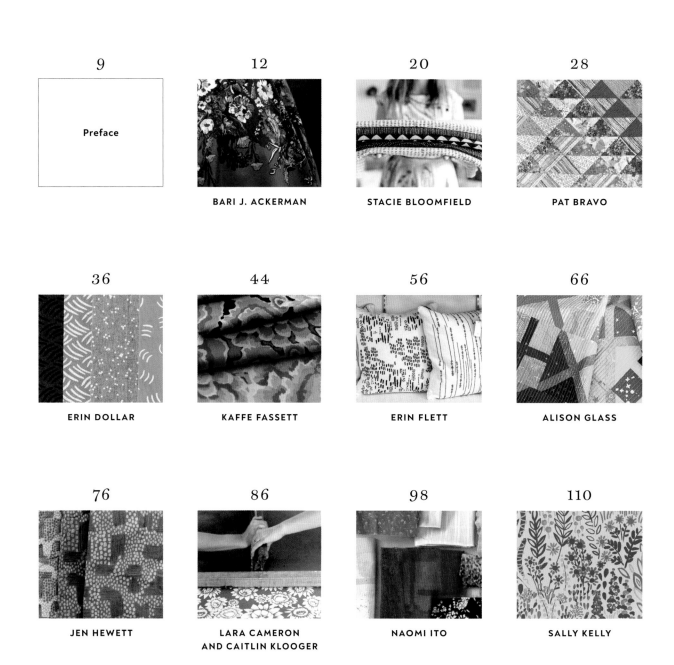

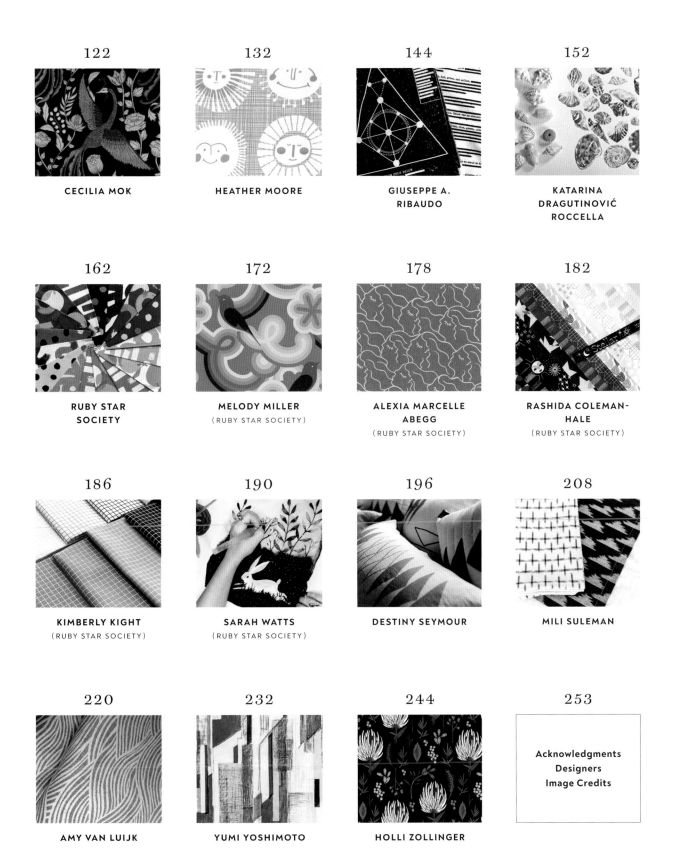

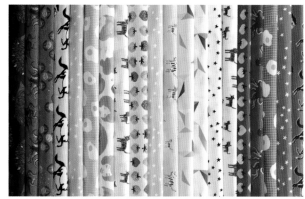

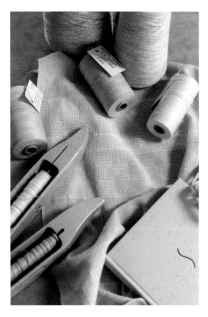

Preface

The journey that culminated in *Modern Fabric* began with a small fabric and art supply store in Belfast, on the coast of Maine. Fiddlehead Artisan Supply is owned and operated by coauthor Abby Gilchrist. Several years ago, our editor, Jan Hartman, walked into Fiddlehead and asked Abby about the fabric that fills the store. Abby replied that she stocks "modern fabric."

As Abby guided her through the shop, Jan pulled bolts from the shelves. "Who designed this fabric?" Alexia Abegg. "And this?" Alison Glass. "And this?" Jen Hewett. The fabrics tell the story of the aesthetic Abby curates for Fiddlehead—what people in the quilting industry call "modern fabric." Solids and textured woven fabrics support the prints. The printed cottons at the front of the shop guide the eye to apparel fabric at the back, including double gauze designed by Naomi Ito of nani IRO and Liberty lawns from Sally Kelly.

After Jan suggested that Abby write a book about these designers, Abby approached Amelia, a textile designer and frequent Fiddlehead customer, to collaborate on the project. While wishing that we (Abby and Amelia) could write about the hundreds of designers whose work we find exciting and inspirational, we had to choose. We wanted to present a diverse group of designers, not just the most established ones or representatives of only one element of the wider fabric industry. In addition, we wanted to feature a range of modern design styles and methods and types of production. We found a broad array: designers who work with fabric companies and those designing independently, those who design for large-scale production, and those who screen print or block print their own designs. But the primary criterion in selecting designers was aesthetic: Would this fabric fit well into Abby's store?

Each essay is based on an interview with the designer. Some interviews were conducted in person and some via video chat; other designers responded to questions in writing. The images accompanying each essay were provided to us or approved by each designer as representative of his or her work.

There is no single definition of "modern fabric." In this book, we let the designers speak about the ideas behind their aesthetic: their inspiration, creative processes, personal opinions, and reflections on design.

OPPOSITE (CLOCKWISE FROM TOP LEFT)
Fabric designed by Holli Zollinger, Ruby Star Society, Lara Cameron and Caitlin Klooger, Sally Kelly, Mili Suleman, and Cecilia Mok
OVERLEAF
Destiny Seymour

The Designers

Bari J. Ackerman

BARI J. DESIGNS
SCOTTSDALE, ARIZONA, USA

Bari J. Ackerman describes her style as "curated maximalism." She loves color, contrast, decor, and design:

> From the time I was a little kid, I've always loved home decor. I always wanted to rearrange my room. My mom would say, "No…!" and then she'd hear me up there, sitting on the floor, pushing with my feet to get the dresser across the room…So, everything, always, was really about decor.

While her daughters were growing up, Bari was a stay-at-home mom. In 2004, she explains, she began making fabric handbags after starting to sew curtains for her house. Bari's bags proved popular, and she sold them via her website and in a dozen boutiques across the country.

By 2008, Etsy had grown in popularity. "There were a million fabric handbags on the market, and everybody was making them out of one particular designer's fabric," Bari says. She wanted to differentiate herself, so she decided to design her own fabric.

"I didn't know how to draw, how to paint, how to do any of that," Bari recalls. She bought an entry-level tablet and started drawing directly in Photoshop. "It took about a year [before] I was finally coming up with designs that I liked, that looked like what I was trying to draw." Her friend, author and fabric designer Jennifer Paganelli, suggested that Bari produce her designs through the recently launched print-on-demand platform Spoonflower. Bari made her printed fabric into a quilt, aprons, and bags and took the designs to the International Quilt Market trade show, where she met representatives of several companies and was offered contracts.

Bari's first collection was launched in 2009 and was followed by four more lines. Two years later, she moved to Pat and Walter Bravo's company, Art Gallery Fabrics, as one of the company's first outside designers. "I think it was kismet; it was exactly the place I needed to be. They are arty and eclectic and encourage out-of-the-box thinking," she says. After several fabric collections with Art Gallery, all designed entirely on the computer, Bari began to paint. "That's when it all changed. I felt like it was what I should be doing. Everything feels a little bit more organic." The first line to include hand-painted designs was her 2014 collection, *Emmy Grace*, a tribute to her daughters.

"The coloring is what makes fabric modern. When you're going with colors that are on trend, everything looks modern and fresh."

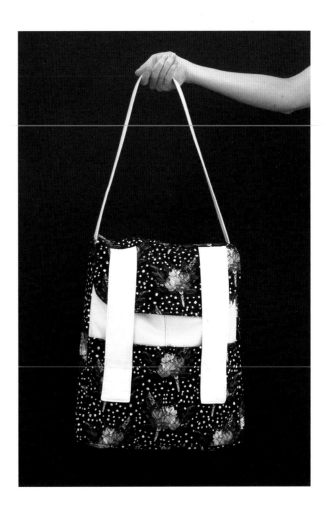

OPPOSITE, TOP
Bari's studio
OPPOSITE, BOTTOM
"Budquette Nightfall" from the
***Emmy Grace* collection**
RIGHT
A bag featuring "West End Blooms"
print from the *Bloomsbury* collection

Bari paints with watercolors, acrylics, and oils. She also incorporates colored pencil drawings. "I paint a lot! I tear out of magazines, I sketch a lot. I paint and draw and paint and draw and paint and draw." When designing a collection, Bari starts with the focal, or "hero," print. She often has a theme in mind but finds that it evolves throughout the design process.

Bari loves flowers and is inspired by nature as well as by various historical eras: "My favorite thing is a period drama movie. I want to watch them over and over and over, but I'm not really watching the movie. I'm looking at the costumes and the sets. I love to go to the theater if I can." Two of Bari's recent collections, Virtuosa and *Bloomsbury*, sprang from these inspirational elements. With *Virtuosa*, Bari conveys the drama of performance in patterns that feature bold blossoms center stage and geometrics and twining leaves in supporting roles. *Bloomsbury* evokes the London gatherings of Virginia Woolf and the Bloomsbury set with subtle references: "There's the boutonniere and some elements that I felt were more high society and some that are more abstract."

LEFT
The *Bloomsbury* collection
RIGHT
A quilt block made with
***Bloomsbury* prints**

"Botanist's Essay" print on rayon,
from the *Bloomsbury* collection

ABOVE
The dining area in Bari's home

RIGHT
A hand-painted mural by Bari

BELOW, LEFT
A rug designed for Bari's *Wild Bloom* collection with Loloi Rugs

BELOW, RIGHT
The *Virtuosa* collection

While Bari closely follows decor trends, her color sense is all her own; she describes her choices as "organic" and "instinctual." In addition to color, Bari often uses different styles and mediums within a fabric line to create contrast and variations in scale:

> If I have a really painty line, then I definitely need to have some digital geometric movements to balance the whole thing out…I always want something that will work as a stripe, then something geometric and digital, a ditsy floral and a large floral, an allover floral, and maybe something more linear…It's usually color that ties it all together.

Bari's artful designs are not restricted to fabric. They can be found on rugs from Loloi, on wallpaper from Wallternatives, and as murals from Murals Your Way. Bari's original paintings and art prints are available, along with pillows and paper goods, on her website. Her blog and social-media posts offer styling techniques and tips for curating a welcoming, colorful, maximalist home. In 2020, Bari released her second book, *Bloom Wild*, which shares her infectious enthusiasm for home decor filled with floral opulence.

LEFT
A quilt made from *Virtuosa* prints
BELOW
A suitcase made with prints from the *Virtuosa* collection

Stacie Bloomfield

GINGIBER
SPRINGDALE, ARKANSAS, USA

Growing up in Springfield, Missouri, Stacie Bloomfield knew she wanted to be an artist. "My earliest memory…is of drawing a bulldog. I was three and wearing a blue leotard. That's how vivid it is." She attended Drury University, graduating with a BA in design and fine arts. Stacie credits her printmaking professor, David Bigelow, as a major influence. "I took every class I could with him. I would skip other classes to go to the printmaking studio. He taught me it was the small details that matter."

Stacie turned to illustration when she was decorating her baby daughter's nursery. She wasn't attracted to "silly-sweet" art for kids and was seeking something that adults could enjoy, too. Stacie drew her own designs and decorated the nursery herself. At her husband's urging, she began to sell the designs on Etsy in 2009.

That's how I started my company, Gingiber. I stole the name off a personal branding project that I did when I was in university. I really liked the lowercase g in one font, [and] I found an old Latin word with repetitive g's: *gingiber*. It means "ginger."

ABOVE, LEFT
Stacie Bloomfield
ABOVE, RIGHT
Llama tea towel

In late 2012, Stacie celebrated three thousand sales on Etsy and in April 2013 launched gingiber.com. As Gingiber grew, Stacie cultivated licensing partnerships with companies such as West Elm, Chasing Paper, and Lulujo. She collaborated with Land of Nod (now Crate&Kids) to design a range of bedding, pillows, towels, chairs, and rugs, launched in 2014, featuring Gingiber's distinctively detailed animal images. Gingiber now offers hundreds of products, such as tea towels, greeting cards, calendars, pillows, art prints, and enamel pins, available on its website and at the studio in Springdale, Arkansas.

LEFT
Gingiber calendar pages
BELOW
Gingiber pillows

Several years later, Stacie "got this bug. It was like a little itch. *I'm just going to design fabric—it's time.*" Initially intending to design home decor fabric, she taught herself to design in repeat and created large floral and animal motifs. Stacie pitched her fabric line to several fabric companies, including Moda Fabrics + Supplies:

> They called back immediately [and] wanted to do something completely different than I had envisioned. I said, "I don't know. Let me think about it." I was so naive. I didn't know that Moda was a big deal. If I had, I might have handled the conversation differently, but I was really honest about what I was thinking and feeling. The next day I called back and said, "Yes!"

LEFT
Gingiber embroidery kits
BELOW
Unicorn tea towel
OPPOSITE, TOP
Prints from *Thicket*
OPPOSITE, BOTTOM
Stacie holding blender prints for *Thicket*, her first collection with Moda Fabrics + Supplies

Stacie works closely with Moda to develop her animal illustrations into full fabric collections. Most of her lines feature four different animal icons with unique visual elements. Stacie uses fur and feather patterns to explore texture, linework, and color. To create blenders and coordinating designs, Stacie collaborates with Moda's design team to extract details from each motif: "In *Thicket* [2016], I had a fox with a bunch of little dashes that represented the fur and an owl with triangles that made up the feathers. We used the dashes and other shapes to make a simple allover repeat for blenders."

Stacie's designs begin with pencil sketches:

I'm a disorganized artist. I don't have a steady sketchbook; I draw on scraps of paper, margins, whatever, and doodle down an idea. My bag is usually filled with little receipts covered in sketches and drawings. Later on, I think, *What was that idea I had?*, and I go through all of my scraps to find that half-baked idea.

Stacie redraws each design using fine-tip gel pens from the Japanese company Muji. They allow her great accuracy when drawing precision design elements. She scans the detailed black-and-white image into Photoshop or Illustrator to "clean it up a bit." If she is working in color, she vectorizes the image and digitally colors the designs before experimenting with scale. "When I was first illustrating…I tried hand printing certain things, but I thought, *I have a kid and there's ink everywhere! This isn't gonna work for me.* So I stopped screen printing and focused on what worked in my environment and [on being] really efficient with my time."

Stacie sketching

"If I focus too much on the end product, I lose the magic…I'm really good at working in the moment."

RIGHT
The Gingiber studio
BELOW
Artwork in progress

Stacie considers herself an illustrator and prefers to create single images, then determine their context, or to develop a product around a motif:

> If I focus too much on the end product, I lose the magic. A lot of times when I'm illustrating, I already have an idea of the shapes I want to use or the impact I want it to have. It's just a matter of sitting down and finding the time to bring it to life. Other times, I let the pen go where it wants to go and see what happens. I'm really good at working in the moment. I just concentrate on finding new ways to use lines, shapes, and texture. Then I find that I have a body of work that is unified, usually accidentally, just by my hands, my linework.

As Gingiber has grown, Stacie has hired support staff to take over customer service, wholesaling, production, and accounting, allowing her the freedom and space to immerse herself in the creative leadership of the company. "When I'm making things for me, doing my own thing, that's what resonates the most with people. I just want to design anything and everything!"

OPPOSITE, TOP
Stacie by her mural
OPPOSITE, BOTTOM
"Be Yourself" art print
RIGHT
The Gingiber studio in Springdale, Arkansas

Pat Bravo

ART GALLERY FABRICS
DANIA BEACH, FLORIDA, USA

Born and raised in Buenos Aires, Argentina, Pat Bravo fell in love
with sewing and knitting at the age of nine. Her mother encouraged
her vivid imagination, busy hands, and tactile nature by enrolling her
in a home economics school. At thirteen, Pat asked to attend an academy
for seamstresses. Despite her mother's reluctance to let her go at such
a young age, Pat spent two years "learning everything about fabrics,
dressmaking, and patterns." She graduated as a fully qualified seamstress
two years later. Pat continued to fashion bespoke garments as she
pursued a more traditional education. After several years of studying
law, she embarked on three years of painting lessons.

   During that time, Pat met Walter Bravo. In 1989, the couple moved
to the United States. Until that time, Pat had never seen a quilt. "When
I saw the magic of the squares and triangles, I said 'I have to do this!'"
She quickly mastered the elements of traditional quilting and dove into
the world of art quilts. Pat recalls:

> I used to do a lot of raw edge appliqué, and I started to do landscapes:…
> rivers, mountains, lakes…At that time, around 1990, there was only a small
> selection of batiks or fabrics that could replicate the trunk of a tree or
> a rock or leaves or bushes. I was feeling very limited. I said, *What if I start
> painting my own fabrics to use in my quilts?* I came out with ranges of
> colors [with] imperceptible differences between one color and the other.

OPPOSITE
Pat Bravo
ABOVE & RIGHT
**Prints from Pat's *Nuncia*
collection**

Pat introduced her painted fabrics at a local quilt guild. The members loved Pat's fabrics because of the subtle tonalities: "warm reds to super-cool reds" and "blue-greens to super-warm greens to almost mustard and olive." She traveled to shows around her home state of Florida and "people went crazy! They started buying it because they didn't see those colors in stores." Pat invited Walter to join her at the International Quilt Festival in Houston. At first he was skeptical about his wife's "hobby," but "when he saw that floor with sixty thousand people, he said, 'This is serious business!'" In Houston Pat was approached by several companies to design fabrics, but Walter said, "No, we will do it ourselves!" Art Gallery Fabrics was born in 2004. The Bravos developed their business without any external financing, a choice that demanded a lot of hard work and sacrifice. Working with mills in South Korea, the Bravos printed Pat's designs on premium cotton. The high thread count (133 by 72 threads per square inch) gives their quilting fabric a silky hand and exceptional drape.

As Art Gallery Fabrics grew, Pat noticed a gap in the industry: "The 'contemporary elegant' was missing. Discerning quilters were looking for something that challenged them, a different print. I saw the gap because I'd been quilting myself for so many years." To provide quilters with sophisticated designs, Pat "started doing two collections a year. And then four collections and six and eight collections a year. From 2004 to 2011, I did this all myself," she says. "But I was getting a little bit tired, and my husband said to me, 'I think it's time to license our first designers.'"

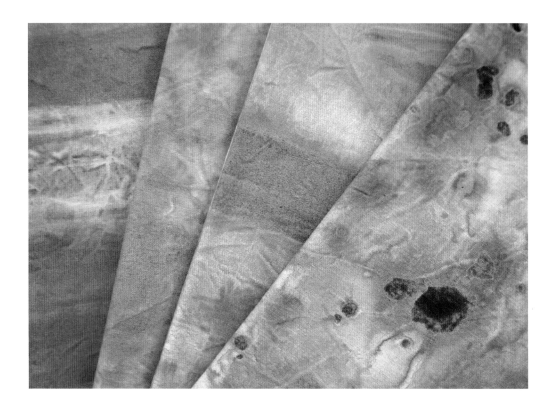

"Modern fabric design is not a word— it is a feeling."

OPPOSITE
Pat's hand-painted fabric
LEFT & BELOW
Pat's studio

In 2019, under Pat's creative leadership and Walter's business guidance, Art Gallery Fabrics released twenty-six collections from twelve designers. Each design must meet Pat's exacting standards: "The print has to make you happy. It has to make you feel young. It has to be chic and elegant; the style doesn't matter."

Although Pat leads the design team at Art Gallery Fabrics and mentors the company's other designers, her own design work is paramount. Since 2004, she has released more than forty collections. The patterns and motifs in Pat's collections focus on a central idea or theme; she begins by creating as many as fifty designs, then selects those that best embody that theme. "When I have that concept in my mind, I start doing drawings of the flowers or the geometric elements. I draw a lot," she says. "In the beginning, I was hand drawing on paper, but now I use my iPad. With Procreate, I have my tablet and my pen; it is a natural way of drawing." She begins with large- and medium-scale focal prints, followed by connector prints and, finally, small prints for blenders. Pat notes that blenders may seem like the easiest element, but "all the dots are made, all the stripes are made; you always have to come up with something that is different. Maybe I find one element of a picture I can convert."

OPPOSITE
Pat Bravo and quilts from her many fabric collections
ABOVE
"Thoughts" quilt, featuring the *Matchmade* **collection**
RIGHT
The *Matchmade* **collection**

Colors, too, can be muses. "I perceive their vibrations. Maybe call me a crazy lady," she laughs. "Red doesn't have the same vibration as blue and so on." For inspiration, Pat travels the world from her studio:

I go to Google and…I hand pick the colors to make me feel like I am in a market in Istanbul or Morocco: bold, saturated, rich colors! Or I can see an ad in a fashion magazine. A few years ago I saw an ad of a lady on the beach. It was done in very pastel colors, peach and aqua—super-soft colors, super-pastel colors…Immediately, I thought, "Oh! This is summer love, all the love of summer!" From that image alone, I created the collection *Summerlove*. I love fashion—I am a fanatic! In 2011 I designed *Rapture*, inspired by Kenzo. It uses beautiful, super-light colors and is very citric.

Pat often works through the night, creating collections to be printed on Art Gallery's quilting fabric, cotton voile, knits, rayon, canvas, and denim. "I live in the night!" she laughs.

Each collection is a child. Each collection has its own process. It has bad moments, ugly moments, exhilarating and beautiful moments. But I do it all with a view of "take comfort, take refuge [in] the beauty that you can make with fabric and a needle and thread."

ABOVE
Summerlove prints in a quilt
RIGHT
A quilt made of prints from *Rapture*

TOP, LEFT

"Wonderlust Bold" print from
Legendary

BOTTOM, LEFT

**Close-up of "Entwine" quilt, made
from Pat's fortieth fabric collection,**
Legendary

TOP, RIGHT

"Femme Metale Boho" print from
Legendary

BOTTOM, RIGHT

The *Legendary* collection

Erin Dollar

COTTON & FLAX
SAN DIEGO, CALIFORNIA, USA

Erin Dollar's life changed forever halfway through her junior year at the University of California at Santa Cruz. As she describes it, she "stumbled into the printmaking department and completely fell in love." As a fine art major, Erin had been honing her sense of design, color, and line, but printmaking captured her "type A, rigorous, analytical side." It was the intersection of scientific thinking—of chemistry and meticulous process—and her artistic style.

Erin graduated in 2008, at the beginning of the recession, and moved back to her home city of Portland, Oregon. She patched together a living working at odd jobs and joined a cooperative printmaking studio housed in a repurposed storage unit, next to the dumpsters in an alley behind a pizza place. In that less-than-glamorous workspace she shared with twenty other artists, Erin found her people—a community of artists who "all had the same weird, shared, very specific interest that was basically a foreign language to everyone else [she] knew."

Erin focused on making art prints on paper and began to print on fabric. She brought "textile experiment pieces" to art sales and sold them on Etsy, where they received a very positive reception. Cotton & Flax made its online debut in 2010. "Then it just overtook my life," laughs Erin. For the first two years, Erin hand printed each piece of fabric at the cooperative studio; sewed finished products; and packaged, labeled, and shipped them from her apartment by herself.

ABOVE
Erin Dollar
OPPOSITE, TOP
"Brushstroke" herringbone pattern from the *Arroyo* collection
OPPOSITE, BOTTOM
***Arroyo* fabrics**

Cotton & Flax expanded when Erin moved to Los Angeles in 2012, found a larger studio space, and connected with sewing collectives to help with production for her growing wholesale business. She launched two collections of products a year with new prints, patterns, and colors and increased her product line from pillows and tea towels to include items such as coasters, napkins, table runners, and lavender sachets.

Erin's work for Cotton & Flax is unified by her single-color designs, printed only in black or white ink on brightly colored base fabric.

When I launched the business, a restricted palette was a way for me to save money on ink, because I only had to buy two colors to create a really diverse product line. I could buy ten different colors of fabric but only make one silk screen. What started as a practical necessity has become my signature style.

The essential elements of Erin's printed patterns are clean, simplified forms, shapes, and lines, often inspired by her sketches: "I try to do some sketching in new places…Something lights up in my creative brain when I'm in front of a new thing." Erin creates drawings for patterns from her collected sketches using rich, black Japanese sumi ink and brushes or pens on smooth Bristol or watercolor paper. She scans the designs into Photoshop or Illustrator to refine them.

LEFT
Erin screen printing fabric for Cotton & Flax in her San Diego studio
ABOVE
"Hills + Valleys" fabric from the *Arroyo* collection
OPPOSITE, TOP
Erin's designs on tea towels for Cotton & Flax
OPPOSITE, BOTTOM
Cotton & Flax pillows

"Modern fabric has very clean design—it's a little bit more minimal. It's sophisticated. Something about it is just a little bit crisper, cleaner."

Erin centers her design process for Cotton & Flax products around the materials: "I named the business, literally, for the fabric: beautiful linen fabrics or cotton/linen blends. I allow the textures and colors of the base fabrics to inform the pattern that I create."

Fabric considerations also led Erin to collaborate with Robert Kaufman Fabrics beginning in 2016. One of her major concerns is "how to offer affordable pieces to as many people as possible without compromising my aesthetics or my ethics in manufacturing," Erin says. She had been using Robert Kaufman *Essex* linen/cotton as a base cloth for products since the early days of Cotton & Flax. "I knew what a beautiful fabric it was, and there was demand, because people were asking me for yardage. 'Can you sell me pieces? Little offcuts?'" Erin pitched her ideas to the Los Angeles–based fabric company. The design team, familiar with Erin's work, collaborated with her to develop colorways but used only her signature black and white ink.

Arroyo, a forty-four-piece collection inspired by the light and textures of the Southern California landscape, was released in 2017. *Balboa*, Erin's second collection of prints on Kaufman's *Essex* linen/cotton, was released in 2018. The second line celebrates the beautifully imperfect nature of the handmade by featuring pattern motifs that echo Anni Albers's weaving, *sashiko* mending techniques, traditional woven basket designs, and spools of thread. Warm neutrals and rich reds and blues with bright green and aqua evoke Erin's adopted home city of San Diego.

RIGHT
Erin beginning new pattern designs with sumi ink
OPPOSITE, TOP
Swatches from the *Balboa* collection
OPPOSITE, BOTTOM
Swatches from the *Arroyo* collection

Shortly after moving from Los Angeles to San Diego in 2017, Erin was forced to stop hand printing because of a back injury:

> I've had to really step back from the manufacturing parts of my business…I'm trying to think about it in a positive way, but it still makes me sad. Printing is the joy of my life. But the reality is that… I needed to become the leader of the company; I really need to be focused on the higher-level creative aspects.

The opportunity to lease a retail space came while Erin was transitioning away from the production and manufacturing side of Cotton & Flax. Erin's brightly lit shop and studio allows her to host small workshops focused on block printing and pattern design. "I get so much joy from teaching because it's kind of rekindling those early memories of connecting with printmaking when I was in college," Erin says. "I'm getting to rediscover the media through the eyes of my students." She also shares the processes used to create designs for Cotton & Flax online. Erin says her students "design their own fabric [and] print it, and then they have made something that's completely unique, completely hand-made…It's empowering."

BELOW
Erin's archive of pattern ideas
OPPOSITE, TOP
Erin in her San Diego studio with the swatch book for the *Arroyo* fabric collection
OPPOSITE, BOTTOM LEFT
Cotton & Flax pillows
OPPOSITE, BOTTOM RIGHT
Swatches of *Balboa* fabric next to Erin's original pattern drawings

Kaffe Fassett

KAFFE FASSETT STUDIO
LONDON, UNITED KINGDOM

"It's all about color! I'm trying to make color as sexy as possible, to make it shine. I'm about glow—that's my purpose in life."

Kaffe Fassett grew up on California's Big Sur coast; his parents owned and operated the famous restaurant Nepenthe, which attracted a bohemian crowd of artists throughout the 1950s. Kaffe and his siblings grew up listening to poets and playwrights and dancing along with performers on the terrace. After studying painting at Boston's School of the Museum of Fine Arts, Kaffe moved to the United Kingdom in 1964. He immediately fell in love with the beauty of wild moorlands and perfectly maintained gardens, humble cottages and stately homes, and with the lived-in antiquity of his chosen home. Kaffe's entrée into making and designing textiles occurred in 1968, when an acquaintance taught him to knit on an overnight train from Inverness to London. Less than a year later, Kaffe began designing for *Vogue Knitting* and was lauded as "the King of Knitting."

ABOVE
Kaffe Fassett in front of a mosaic made by Brandon Mably
OPPOSITE
Kaffe Fassett Collective quilting prints

His bold, often unconventional colors and patterns became wildly popular. Over the next twenty-five years, Kaffe designed and created knits, needlepoint, tapestries, mosaics, paintings, and dance and theater costumes. He frequently drew inspiration for knitting patterns from English and American antique quilts but never ventured into the world of patchwork or printed cottons.

Kaffe first met Liza Prior Lucy, a US rep for Rowan yarns, in the early 1990s. As their friendship blossomed, Liza told Kaffe, "You are going to design for patchwork." She gradually dragged Kaffe "kicking and screaming" into the world of patchwork by making tiny quilts out of his knitted designs and mailing them across the Atlantic. Kaffe replied to Liza with comments and suggested changes. "See, you're designing!" she exclaimed.

Kaffe was hooked. Large quilts provided a canvas on which to expand and amplify his use of color. While sewing quilts with Liza for their first patchwork book, *Glorious Patchwork: More Than 25 Glorious Quilt Designs*, published in 1998, they encountered a lack of cotton prints to fulfill the exotic designs in Kaffe's imagination: "Where [was] the big paisley or the big bouquet of flowers? Everything was tiny little prints. Cute was rampant." He explains that his original goal "was to bring the Old World to life…all of that rich pattern-on-pattern…and rich use of color. I've moved from a very, very painterly baroque kind of style to something that's increasingly more graphic."

OPPOSITE
Kaffe's artwork drawer
RIGHT
Kaffe working on his *Shot Cottons* range for Free Spirit Fabrics

Kaffe finds design inspiration in everything from ancient frescoes and mosaics to historical and ethnic textiles to "a fabulous [bunch] of flowers…Each one is kind of a circle, but there's a lot of complexity within the circle. Sometimes [there are] lots of little petals; sometimes it's just a big blob of circularness. And then maybe there's a big geranium leaf…I draw it flower by flower and just build up this series of circles."

In 2006, Kaffe added fabric designs by Philip Jacobs to his collections. Jacobs draws inspiration from archives of early English and French textiles and wallpaper to paint exquisitely detailed botanical, feather, and shell patterns. Each year Kaffe combs through his latest portfolio of paintings and makes selections that fit with his upcoming ranges. By 2008, the Kaffe Fassett Collective fabric lines had expanded to include designs by Brandon Mably. An acclaimed knitwear designer and author, Brandon travels the world teaching knitting and color workshops in addition to managing Kaffe's London studio. Mably's vibrant, playful fabric designs are deeply inspired by the people and communities he visits. Kaffe guides the color palette and style of each release and says, "I feel at times like a movie director who has a favorite team for film after film."

"Enchanted"
prints in different
colorways

LEFT
"Enchanted" artwork and needlepoint
BELOW
"Enchanted" artwork in progress

A self-proclaimed Luddite, Kaffe eschews the use of computers; he recounts his only experience with one:

> I was doing coloring for Philip Jacobs, and I thought I had to do [that] on the computer, because how could I sit and actually paint out every color if we're doing these big collections?…And so I hired, at great expense, a girl to computerize the coloring…It was very difficult to do, and I didn't particularly like the results. I sat down one day and just started painting them out. It was quicker, much cheaper, and more direct. And my inspiration came through my hand in painting. So I thought, *To hell with that!* and I've done it by hand ever since.

LEFT
"Row Flowers" prints in different colorways
ABOVE
Artwork for "Row Flowers"

Kaffe Fassett and Brandon Mably
working in their studio

TOP
**Fabric from the Kaffe Fassett
Collective, designed by Philip Jacobs,
Brandon Mably, and Kaffe Fassett**
BOTTOM
**Kaffe Fassett, Liza Prior Lucy, and
Brandon Mably**
OPPOSITE
Shelves of fabric in the Kaffe Fassett Studio

Kaffe draws out a pattern repeat with a pencil and fills in the colors using a small paintbrush and gouache, an opaque watercolor. Each of six colorways in a collection is painted over a color photocopy of the first, translating each color from one version to the next. Finished designs are sent to the printer, and samples, called "strike-offs," are returned. Although Kaffe meticulously colors each element by hand, there are still surprises when the print comes back. "Oh, my God! This color! I wasn't even dreaming it would look like it does!…Or maybe a green doesn't work because it's suddenly on a blue flower. Then I can have a second chance, but more often than not, the first strike-off is fine because I really thought about it." Kaffe's passion for color is evident as he describes "wonderful, smoldering colors": wine reds, mysterious purple-blues, rich ambers, and lighter shades of "mossy greens and buffy browns."

The process does not end when the fabric designs are submitted to the printer. Kaffe, Brandon, and Liza then create their quilt patterns by deliberately cutting pieces containing specific elements of each fabric and sticking them to a design wall. They carefully arrange the pieces by hand; nothing is designed on the computer. "A design or a textile has to have life," says Kaffe. "Things that are too perfect are just lifeless and boring…bloodless." When a collection of quilts is complete, Kaffe and his team travel to stunning locations to photograph them, the most recent being Burano, an island in the Venetian Lagoon, with its brightly colored fishermen's cottages. These settings "make the colors in each quilt come alive because [the quilt] responds to the background…I'm constantly echoing colors in my photographs."

Crucial to Kaffe's sense of color and pattern is contrast. "Sometimes you want quite hard contrast—sharp, so that it's kind of dancing. But if you have too much contrast, you kill the shine. A lot of quilts are very high contrast, and the color is thrown out the window." Kaffe explains that the use of black and white can disrupt the color nuances, harmonies, and vibrations, leaving only light and dark forms yet little glow. Even so, some of his favorite quilts use black and white prints to stunning effect. "Color affects us so emotionally. The right placement of color and proportion achieves a harmony that, like a good work of art, has the power to appeal down through the centuries."

ABOVE
A few of Kaffe's prints
RIGHT
Kaffe Fassett
OPPOSITE
**Kaffe painting the cupboards
in his living room**

Erin Flett

GORHAM, MAINE, USA

Immediately upon graduating from the University of Kansas with a BFA in graphic design, Erin Flett "U-Hauled it east" with two dogs, a cat, and her fiancé, Maslen, to Portland, Maine, where her parents had retired. Her first four years in Portland were spent working for an advertising agency, where she quickly advanced to the position of art director. In part "because nobody had any money to buy photos," Erin says, she often added small hand-drawn embellishments to wedding invitations, catalogs, and brochures. Her drawings delighted her clients; these motifs were the beginning of Erin's hand-drawn style.

When Erin was expecting her first child, she began building a successful business as a freelance graphic designer. Yet she longed to create her own designs and traveled to the Surface Design Show in New York to investigate selling her work. Through contacts she made there, she started producing designs for companies like Pottery Barn Teen. But the companies she was working with were asking for "super-safe" patterns. "That made me realize that no one was going to do my aesthetic," she explains.

OPPOSITE
Erin Flett
ABOVE
Pillows by Erin Flett

Erin designed her first pillow as a wedding present, but she didn't know how to screen print. She took her design to a local T-shirt company: "As soon as they printed it, something happened. It was like a light bulb went off—it resonated instantly!...I could put my designs on fabric! It was so fast; it was instant gratification." For the next year, Erin created designs that could be printed with small screens. She mixed her inks at home and brought the designs and fabric to the T-shirt shop. Finally, the owner said, "Erin, this is crazy! You need to learn how to print."

Erin began printing with her husband, Maslen, in the basement of their home, when their daughters were two and five. To maximize their small space, Maslen, a carpenter, built racks that hoist printed fabric above the table to dry while Erin printed more pieces. To meet demand for the line of pillows in her Etsy shop, she hired her first employee, a printer who is still part of her team. After two years of working in her basement, Erin was featured in a full-page profile in *O, The Oprah Magazine*. The extraordinary publicity gave her the confidence to move her operation to a studio space on the fourth floor of a former cotton mill overlooking the Presumpscot River in Westbrook, Maine, where the business continued to expand for the next seven years. In 2019, Erin and her team moved to a new location that is four times the size of the previous studio. Located in a corner building in downtown Gorham, Maine, the new manufacturing space includes a showroom and retail space.

"Modern fabric design is an interpretation of one's own life and experiences. Good design tells a story."

LEFT
A few of Erin's bucket hats
OPPOSITE
A display in the showroom
OVERLEAF
The busy and highly organized workroom

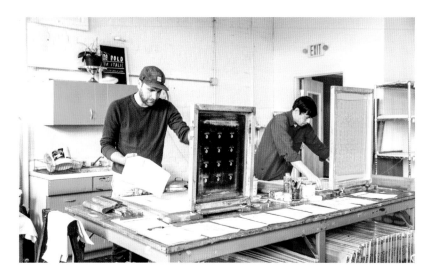

ABOVE AND RIGHT
**Screen printing fabrics for
a week's orders**
BELOW, LEFT
**Hanging the screen-printed
fabrics up to dry**
BELOW, RIGHT
Screen-printed fabrics

Over the years, Erin's offerings for wholesale and retail customers grew to include hundreds of hand-printed designs on a wide range of pillows and bags, hats, and goods for the table and kitchen, such as tea towels, napkins, and glassware. She has also introduced wallpaper and custom yardage options for trade and hospitality customers, and she recently finished designs for a three-hundred-room hotel in California. Her design and printing methods, however, have changed little. The majority of Erin's products are still printed on cut fabric using small screens.

All orders are carefully organized to flow through the studio's production line. The studio manager creates a detailed list for each order, which is sent to the cutters, who prepare pieces of cloth for specific products. The cuts are passed to the printers, who screen print each piece by hand following the image and color specifications on the print list. The prints are then hung to dry on laundry-style lines before being sent to the stitchers, who sew the finished products. "We are a made-to-order design studio. Our whole model is that we only print, sew, and make what is already sold. We don't really have any inventory, and it works brilliantly because we don't have to invest in what's not selling…The team prints about 150 to 200 pieces a day." Erin's stitchers are all local women and men who work from home or in the studio. Of her team, Erin says, "I'm surrounded by amazing people who really believe in our process and craft."

Nearly all of Erin's base cloths are woven in America. She works closely with cotton mills in North Carolina that produce cotton canvas and bark cloth, a tightly woven cotton fabric with a textured crepe weave. "I love the aesthetic of linen and our textured cottons…All of my cottons are woven in the United States. I get my linen from a mill in Belgium; they have a huge range of weights…The fabric has to have a special feeling to it; it has to have a soul."

LEFT
One of the stitchers at work in the studio
ABOVE
Samples of Erin Flett's designs

Erin's deep involvement in every aspect of her business leaves limited time for creating designs. Twice a year, Erin immerses herself in drawing and designing. She usually starts out with an idea or an image and makes thousands of sketches, doodles, drawings, and paintings before selecting specific images that resonate with her. Sometimes she will use a piece of artwork as a whole design, but more often, she cuts up her drawings and collages them together. Erin calls on her graphic design skills to transform her initial hand drawings by copying, pasting, flipping, and repeating them on the computer.

I can be inspired by anything, whether I'm going for a walk with my kids or gardening; I take pictures all the time…Everything I see becomes a pattern. I was running with a friend and had to stop to take a picture of the way the light was going through the leaves; there was the most beautiful pattern on the ground…Artists and designers have brains that are naturally like a kind of sieve; all this information comes in, and we have this innate need to create pattern and design.

BELOW
Erin Flett dopp kits
OPPOSITE, TOP
Erin Flett pillows in the showroom
OPPOSITE, BOTTOM LEFT
**Products showing the wide range
of made-to-order prints and colors**
OPPOSITE, BOTTOM RIGHT
Erin in her studio

Alison Glass

YORKTOWN, VIRGINIA, USA

When Alison Glass's children were three and five, her husband went back to school to get his PhD, and Alison started a home-decoration and organization business. Within a year, she had left behind the organization services in favor of project management. Working closely with clients, Alison created custom looks for new or remodeled spaces, including sewing and reupholstery projects. "I was using fabric from the quilt industry—mostly from FreeSpirit, because they were the ones doing home decor weight," she says. "I became fascinated with the idea of designing fabric; the elements of color and repeat especially appealed to me."

As her husband neared the completion of his dissertation, Alison designed several fabric lines. "It was a challenge to figure out how to present them to manufacturers. I didn't really know people in the industry." Alison decided to attend International Quilt Market, where she met with several fabric companies. After careful consideration, she signed with Andover Fabrics and worked closely with art director Kathy Hall: "She was my biggest mentor in terms of how fabric actually gets made and how to design in a way that works." Alison's first collection, *Lucky Penny*, was launched in 2012.

OPPOSITE
Fabric from Alison Glass's collection *Seventy Six*
ABOVE, LEFT
Prints from Alison's *Handiwork* **collection**
ABOVE, RIGHT
Alison Glass

When designing, Alison begins with a theme. "Not a theme like 'elephants'; it's more what I'm thinking about. It probably has more to do with thoughts than visuals." Some themes are layered and deeply personal; others are inspired by the exquisite details of the natural world as well as the man-made. "Making a conscious decision to see those beautiful elements creates a nearly endless stream of ideas and thoughts. I love the process of taking these glimpses and translating them into my own ideas, colors, and patterns."

Alison's lines are typically named before they are drawn. She begins with lists of design ideas and colors, working to develop her theme, then enhances the lists with simple sketches: "just enough to get the right shapes and lines." Her first real designs are drawn on tracing paper, where she refines the lines and gets a sense of the repeat. "Fabric is weird. You can have a small element of a theme, but it becomes a bigger thing when you repeat the design across the fabric." Once she gets immersed in drawing details, Alison says, she "can't stop!"

When layer upon layer of tracing paper drawings reveals the final repeated motif, Alison takes a photo with her phone and uploads it to Illustrator, where she retraces the design. "Then I do some color work on the computer," she explains, "not to perfect it, but to get an idea of what I want. Once I know where all the color placements are within the repeated design, I send it to Andover."

ABOVE, LEFT
The *Road Trip* collection
ABOVE, RIGHT
Charlotte City Tote by Alicia Miller of Swoon Patterns, made from Alison's "Art Theory" panel from her *Ex Libris* collection
RIGHT
A pillow made from Alison's *Insignia* collection, a rainbow palette with small scattered prints
OPPOSITE
The *Sun Print Light* collection

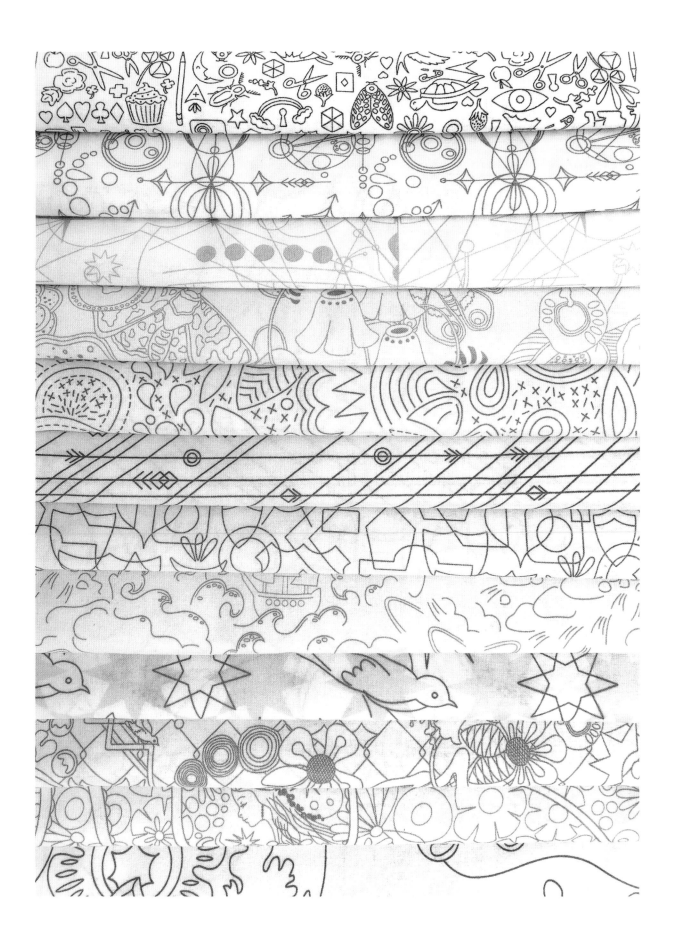

TOP
"Bungalow" quilt pattern from Alison Glass's *Insignia* collection, quilted by Gina Pina
BOTTOM LEFT
Prints from *Road Trip*
BOTTOM RIGHT
Alison selecting colors for her prints

The team at Andover digitally isolates the color areas and returns the design to Alison. She makes selections from the "kajillion colors that are possible with the printing system," to translate the colors in her imagination and on her computer screen into information for the mill. "Fabric is not flat; it has texture. It looks different because of how the light hits it." Alison sends her color selections back to the company, where a sample is printed. The process may be repeated several times to achieve the perfect palette. "I love the system," Alison laughs. "It allows me to be highly controlling, which is apparently my favorite thing to be."

While Alison refers to herself as "a super-boring dresser," preferring gray, black, and brown to brighter shades, the colors she uses in her work are vivid and saturated.

> I want the colors to be sophisticated and to last. I do colors [that] tend to be a little offbeat…Nothing is just red or just blue—it's a few steps away from those colors. With highly saturated colors, you need other colors that are super-dull and pukey to make the saturated colors look really good. The contrast makes the brighter colors shine.

The *Handiwork* collection

In addition to her print collections, Alison has developed three extensive coordinating lines of fabric: *Mariner Cloth*, *Kaleidoscope*, and *Handcrafted*. *Mariner Cloth*, a yarn-dyed cotton, adds texture to her fabric line and color palette. Each colorway uses only two colors, with alternating widths of textured weft stripes that highlight the contrasts.

Kaleidoscope is a range of shot cotton fabrics. Two distinct colors are woven together: one in the warp, the other in the weft. These intersecting colors create a third color, and as the cloth moves, the two-tone shadowing creates depth. In order to create the 40 fabrics in the line in shades consistent with her color palette, Alison sent more than 150 color combinations to the mill. "It's a huge guessing game to know how two colors are going to look when you put them together in that manner.…It took almost a year to get the colors right."

BELOW
Mariner Cloth, a textured woven fabric line

RIGHT
A quilt displaying *Observatory*, one of Alison's batik collections

Handcrafted is a modern interpretation of batik fabric made using a traditional process. Skilled artisans in Indonesia stamp designs in wax on undyed or colored fabric to create a "resist" where the original color of the cloth will remain distinct after the piece is overdyed. Each bolt of fabric is produced individually; the many hands crafting the cloth imbue the designs with perfectly imperfect variations.

"I want the colors to be sophisticated and to last. I do colors that tend to be a little offbeat…Nothing is just red or just blue."

ABOVE
A quilt made from
Handcrafted 1 & 2
RIGHT
Alison working with samples
of her fabric lines

For Alison, running her business is key. "I'm definitely not sitting around drawing all day. I spend much more time running the business and marketing than I do designing, but that's starting to shift because I don't have enough time to do everything." Alison's brand has expanded from fabric design and collaborations with quilting and sewing pattern designers to other products that feature her surface designs. "The artwork morphs…I've changed the way I draw lines because I want the lines themselves to be more usable for other products, such as embroidery patterns, gift wrap, notecards, enamel pins, and art prints."

When designing, Alison is extremely conscious of the end use of her fabric: "I'm not creating a finished item; I'm creating material for somebody else to use. If I don't do that in a way that is easy for them to translate into their own projects, then it's not a great line." Alison aims to create designs with timeless qualities. She wants to produce materials that are worthy of the time and effort it takes to create something by hand, materials that embody her company's motto: *Beautiful, useful, high-quality design.*

OPPOSITE
The "Lumen" quilt, a pattern designed by Nydia Kehnle for Alison Glass using Alison's collection *Sun Print 2019.* **Color layout design by Alison Glass, pieced by Kelley Paz, and quilted by Gina Pina**

RIGHT
Alison's *Sun Print 2019* **collection**

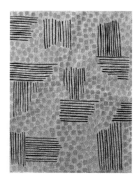

Jen Hewett

SAN FRANCISCO, CALIFORNIA, USA

Jen Hewett found her way into the world of print when she needed
a creative outlet while working at a corporate job: "On a whim, I decided
to take a screen-printing class. I ended up falling in love." That experience
led her to explore other forms of printmaking. From 2008 to 2010, Jen
sold her prints on paper at craft fairs. "People would come up to me and
say, 'I really love this print, but I don't know what to do with it. I'll have
to go home and frame it, and I don't know where it will go.'" Jen saw
that many of her compatriots in craft were making bags; but everyone
seemed to be using the same types of quilting prints. She began to print
her own fabric and sewed her hand-printed cloth into bags for several
years. Eventually she moved away from printing yardage and doing all
of the sewing herself in favor of printing on premade items, such as linen
tea towels for her Tea Towel of the Month Club.

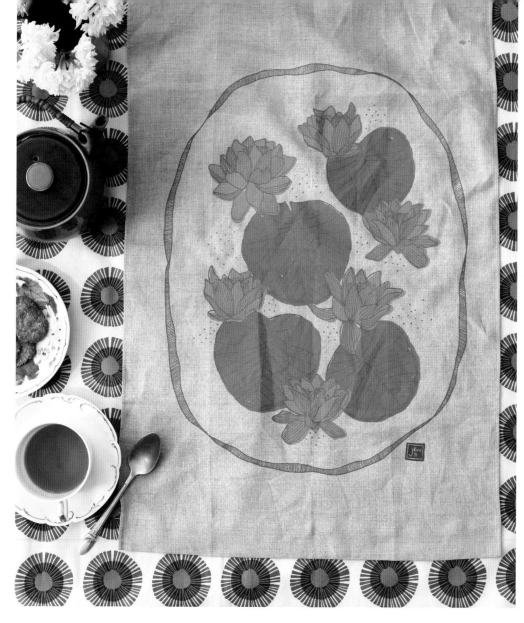

OPPOSITE, LEFT
Jen Hewett
OPPOSITE, RIGHT
**Screen-printed linen: "Imaginary Basket,"
"Dot Square Dash," "Bunch of Squares,"
and "Two-Toned Mountains"**
ABOVE
**"Water Lilies" tea towel, featuring
a three-color hand screen print on linen**
RIGHT
**"Florence" pillow, featuring a three-
color hand screen print on linen**

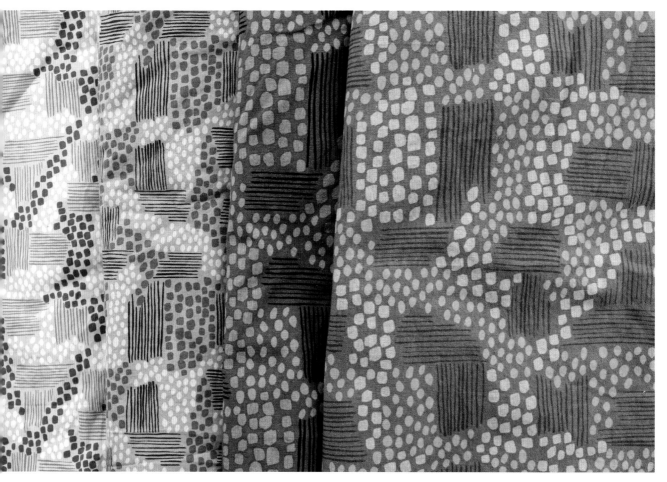

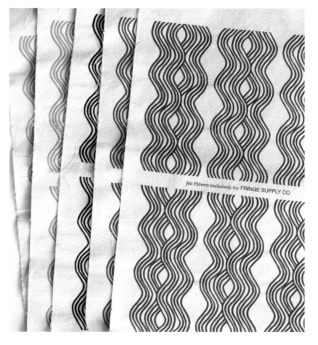

TOP
"Aerial View" fabric with
Cotton+Steel in (left to right)
Sand, Stone, Midnight, and Siesta

BOTTOM, LEFT
"Stone Path" fabric in Rose Gold
from *Imagined Landscapes* collection
with Cotton+Steel

BOTTOM, RIGHT
Custom colorways for the "Hank" bag,
a collaboration with Fringe Supply Co.

Customers frequently ask Jen to sell hand-printed yardage, but it is often impractical, in part because printing large pieces is an extremely labor-intensive process. The best way to make her designs available to as many people as possible is through licensing. Jen's collection of commercially available yardage, *Imagined Landscapes*, was released in 2018 with Cotton+Steel. The line of twenty-two pieces on unbleached quilting cotton and linen/cotton canvas distills the landscape and flora of her native California into layered, "quirky, geometric shapes." The designs capture the essence of the hand-printed images Jen created with block and screen printing.

Jen also collaborated with Fringe Supply Co. to print canvas for limited-edition Field Bags. They were a huge hit, but because she was hand printing, they were inherently small-batch. To ensure ongoing availability, Jen licensed a design to Fringe that can be made by another printer.

As a child and teenager, Jen was drawn to textiles by Marimekko and Vera Neumann:

This was work that was maybe twenty or thirty years old, but it felt really fresh and not overdone like a lot of things in the 1970s and '80s. It was very clean and modern. Vera Neumann actually started out by printing her own scarves on parachute silk in the '40s, during rationing. It's really hard to print on silk; a lot of her work is very off register, misaligned. She had to compensate for the fact that she was printing by herself on very slippery fabric. A lot of my work is still off register, precisely because I'm printing by hand. When you have a machine, you don't have to worry about it.

RIGHT
"Mountains" limited-edition Field Bags for Fringe Supply Co., one-color screen print on cotton canvas
OVERLEAF
Jen's inspiration wall

Jen's designs often begin with sketches inspired by long walks with her energetic dog through Golden Gate Park and the surrounding hills.

I have a big table in my studio that faces outside. I have a lot of light in that room…I tend to reference clippings a lot—I don't use Pinterest very often. I'll clip out things from a piece of paper, from magazines, wrapping paper,…or packaging. I just tack everything up on my board. There's not always a central theme; in fact, there almost never is. It's just a series of impressions….Taking that in every single day means that when I actually sit down to draw, I've soaked in all of this stuff. I'm a sponge, and it's going to come back out of me.

Jen scans her hand-drawn images into Photoshop to experiment with color and layout. She then prints out the design elements and tiles the pieces of paper together before tracing the final design by hand onto film. Jen could have her screen films digitally made, but she feels that working too extensively in Photoshop or Illustrator can make the designs look too polished: "My work is…a little bit wonky. Even when I clean things up in Photoshop, it doesn't look too perfect… It looks like a human being did it…That's one of the big differences between my work and a lot of other surface design."

"I don't try to create realistic drawings. Rather, I try to capture each item's essence, revealing just enough to evoke it."

LEFT
Jen sketching in Procreate
ABOVE
"Fern Dell" fabric in Navy (left) and Rose Gold (right), from *Imagined Landscapes*

Jen's collection with Cotton+Steel was based almost exclusively on her block printed designs. To create repeats for yardage, Jen printed the images in black ink as many as a dozen times, achieving different levels of "wonkiness," as she terms it. The combined prints were scanned into the computer and put into repeat.

Jen's favorite themes are nature, botanicals, geometrics, or a combination of all three. She often starts with the most complex design of a collection, which might be an elaborate floral motif, followed by geometric or striped coordinates. "I don't do the little dots and smaller kinds of ditsy prints. They are almost all focal prints; they shouldn't all work together, but somehow they do."

ABOVE
Ink drawings on vellum for Jen's 2018 tea towels

RIGHT
"Paperwhites" tea towel, a three-color hand screen print on linen

Saturated colors in offbeat combinations also distinguish Jen's work. "I often choose colors that my mother would say don't go together, and I make them go together." When designing for Cotton+Steel, Jen worked with her own colors and then tweaked them to coordinate with the more extensive line. For her most recent Tea Towel of the Month Club project, Jen used a predetermined color palette to focus her designs:

> I had a theme. I had…two greens that I knew I had to work with. So every flower had to work with one of those two greens. And I had three different grays…I used to do everything free form on my own and have no restrictions; it's actually nice to have restrictions.

In addition to her printing, surface design, and licensing work, Jen teaches block-printing and screen-printing classes online, across the United States and in Jaipur, India, through a travel company. She dreams of one day having a fully licensed line of housewares and soft goods, encompassing all kinds of things for the home, and perhaps even clothing inspired by Marimekko's bold prints and subtle branding.

Jen has lived in San Francisco her entire adult life and acknowledges the challenges of being an independent artist in an expensive city. Still, she resists the option of working as an in-house designer for a large company:

> I was always really clear that I wanted my work to be my own and that I didn't want to have to chase after trends. But the decision to remain independent means that there are certain insecurities. I worked doing HR consulting for six years part-time so that I could develop a body of work. I have a vision of what I want to do, what I want to put out there in the world. So when it's accepted, that's a wonderful feeling…I feel so much that the work I'm doing is an extension of me.

LEFT
Jen's studio wall
ABOVE
"Headlands" design in Midnight from
Imagined Landscapes
OPPOSITE
"Superbloom" design in Sunset from
Imagined Landscapes

Lara Cameron
and Caitlin Klooger

INK & SPINDLE
MELBOURNE, AUSTRALIA

Lara Cameron and Caitlin Klooger are the team behind Ink & Spindle. Passionately inspired by the Australian landscape and its flora and fauna, they create planet-friendly, timeless, screen-printed textiles.

Lara, who studied web and graphic design, changed career paths when she began to seek something more tactile: "I like the challenges of printed-pattern design. I like the combination of creative and technical skills. I just started experimenting with patterns. I had a craft blog when they were all the rage, before Instagram." At the time, Lara was not yet printing her own cloth but used another print studio and sold her fabrics on Etsy.

"I was doing the same thing," says Caitlin. "I was in landscape architecture but didn't want to go back to it after a maternity leave." While at home with two babies, Caitlin started designing, found a printer, and sold her fabrics online. Caitlin and Lara got to know each other at trade shows but did not work together for another five years.

OPPOSITE
"Flowering Gum" print
ABOVE, LEFT
Lara Cameron and Caitlin Klooger
ABOVE, RIGHT
A range of prints and colors by Ink & Spindle

Lara cofounded Ink & Spindle with other partners in 2008. When two members of the original trio left to pursue different dreams, Lara and Caitlin joined forces. "I was still really excited and keen to keep going, and it was so good when Caitlin came on board. She had fresh energy and enthusiasm!"

The partners work together on all aspects of the business. "Yeah," Lara laughs, "we try to share the fun jobs and the crap jobs. We've got complementary qualities. Caitlin's a bit more like, *Let's just get it done!*, and I'm a bit more of a perfectionist. We meet in the middle, and it's a good middle."

"I think we're lucky we found each other, because we have similar tastes and styles and aesthetics," adds Caitlin.

In 2018, Ink & Spindle relocated its studio to the Abbotsford Convent arts precinct, less than two and a half miles (four kilometers) from Melbourne's central business district. The protected heritage site hosts more than a hundred artists, wellness practitioners, and community organizations. Caitlin and Lara's space accommodates their 42.6-foot (13-meter) print table, studio equipment, and workshop plus room to spare for a retail space, where they offer customers ready-made home goods and fabric yardage.

Printing with screens measuring 5.9 feet (1.8 meters) tall requires two people at all times. While Ink & Spindle employs several part-time staff members and hosts interns, Lara and Caitlin are always part of the printing team: "There's a lot we've learned over the years…how many passes of the squeegee, which squeegee to use, and how the different base cloths influence that," Caitlin explains. "There are a lot of things that we kind of know subliminally."

RIGHT
"Bracken" print hanging to dry above "Flowering Gum"
OPPOSITE, ABOVE AND BOTTOM RIGHT
Lara (left) and Caitlin printing together
OPPOSITE, BOTTOM LEFT
Caitlin hoisting the fabric
OVERLEAF
Three of Ink & Spindle's screens for printing

"The limitations of screen printing help with the design," Caitlin says. "You can focus on the design—it gives you structure." Most Ink & Spindle fabric prints use only two colors, but some "overprinted artworks," created specifically as wall art, use as many as sixteen layers of color. Each color in a design requires a different screen, representing one layer or part of an overall pattern; the images on the screens tessellate to make a seamless repeat. Through overprinting, screen flips, and displacements, Lara and Caitlin can create a range of patterns from a single screen.

"It's about being clever with our processes. We work with a limited color palette and very simplistic equipment," says Lara.

"[We] keep our palette fairly restrained because we like to be able to reuse the same colors, not have to be constantly mixing up new colors. We keep it quite harmonious and work within that; we have a palette of colors we love, and the whole palette looks good together," adds Caitlin.

The inks used at Ink & Spindle are water based and certified organic but are only available in a "bright, vivid, vibrant palette." Caitlin and Lara use those pigments to create their own palette by mixing colors and adding extender to make the ink more transparent, "knocking it back, bringing it to a more natural color." Using thinned ink allows the base fabric to be visible beneath the printing, incorporating the beauty of the organic cotton, eco-linen, or hemp cloth as part of the design.

LEFT
"Hakea" print
ABOVE
"Bottlebrush" print

Making customized fabrics for interiors is a large part of Ink & Spindle's business. Clients can select a base cloth, a design, and colors to create the perfect fabric:

> Allowing people to customize means that they're involved in part of the design—then they have ownership of that piece…They're really thinking about the context and choosing something that they feel is going to be timeless and classic…because what we produce isn't cheap. Part of our ethos is producing something that has longevity. It's less about trends; it's more about slow design, thoughtful design, and a timeless color palette.

Custom-mixed inks

Lara and Caitlin work together in every aspect of their business except for the initial development of design ideas. They both prefer to work alone and be in "their own little world." Lara often records inspiration through her photography: "I might see a leaf or a branch or a little bit of fern and think, *I really like that*. I take a photo and manipulate the image to turn it into a screen. By the time you get to the end result, you almost can't tell it was a photo." Caitlin uses a similar route from inspiration to finished print by recording her inspiration in drawings and watercolor paintings. She transforms the whole image—or a particular element or texture—into a repeat pattern on the computer.

"Often an idea brews for a long time," says Lara. "Sometimes it can take a year or more to finally figure [it] out…And then other times you just do a quick sketch and that's it!"

"We don't collaborate on designs as much as we discuss and develop…One of us will have the original design idea, but we work quite collaboratively in terms of what colors to print and what cloth to print on and how to turn it into a reality," says Caitlin.

OPPOSITE
Ink & Spindle's showroom is at the end of the studio
BELOW
Prints by Ink & Spindle (clockwise from top left): "Kurrajong," "Kangaroo Paw," "Spotted Quoll," "Budgie and Banksia"

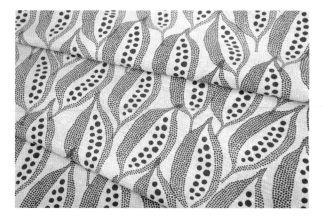

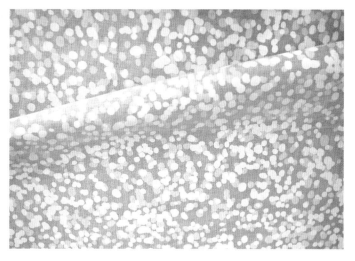

Lara and Caitlin acknowledge the challenges of producing hand-printed, environmentally friendly fabrics in a world of mass production—particularly the financial costs of materials and labor. They are heartened, however, by the fact that consumers are increasingly considering the provenance of fabrics. "People are now thinking more about the process," Caitlin observes. "*Where does it come from? Who made it?* They're wanting to have a little bit more of the story behind it. They want to be engaged with it."

"Another problem is time and excitement management!" Caitlin and Lara laugh. "We've just got so many ideas…We have to funnel it down!"

Lara and Caitlin fully embrace their goals for Ink & Spindle: "We can't imagine being part of some big, giant enterprise where everything is done by somebody else…We're always refining what we do, making it more amazing, more beautiful, more polished, more environmentally friendly—just building on all of the things that we're doing at the moment."

"Modern fabric design is about being timeless, classic, and ethical; the provenance of the fabric is part of the story."

OPPOSITE, TOP
Ink & Spindle's showroom
OPPOSITE, BOTTOM
"Everlasting" in Yellow Ochre
RIGHT
Caitlin and Lara hoisting fabric to dry

Naomi Ito

NAOMI ITO TEXTILE
NANI IRO
OSAKA, JAPAN

Naomi Ito reads the poetry of nature and translates it into designs on cloth. She learned to draw by studying the pictures on the walls of cafés or the murals in stores and continued her practice through college classes. She originally intended to be a picture-book author and illustrator and showed her work for the first time in 1994, at exhibitions in Osaka, Tokyo, and Paris. Several years later, she assembled a portfolio of her art for submission to publishers. A friend passed the portfolio on to Kokka, a textile manufacturer in Osaka, and she was soon offered a job there in textile design. While she was considering the offer from Kokka, her mother shared the fact that her grandfather had been a textile designer, providing the impetus for Naomi to embark on her career in textiles.

In 2002, her brand for Kokka, nani IRO, made its debut. *Nani*, from the Hawaiian language, means "beauty" or "splendor," and *iro* (色) is the Japanese word for "color" and "harmony." Through nani IRO, Naomi has released at least 800 specific colorings of more than 175 designs. Her annual collection launches in February each year.

OPPOSITE
nani IRO 2019 spring release
ABOVE, LEFT
Naomi Ito
ABOVE, RIGHT
Fabric samples and clothing featuring Naomi's prints "Lei Nani" and "Fuccra: Rakuen"

"Rakuen, a world where flowers and birds sing, overflowing with light."

Naomi's home is surrounded by nature, and she takes inspiration each day from the morning light. Her family owns a small organic orchard, where herbs are grown under the trees. "The movements of my brush are inspired by the growing process of the fruits or plants, with changing colors day by day," Naomi says. She translates impressions from her five senses into drawings: "The motifs are based on daily life and range from the shapeless, such as the feeling of the air or gradations of light and mist, to defined shapes, such as flowers or fruits that I grow."

"Our textiles are treated as a single work of art that uses graphic compositions to fully express its beauty and features color schemes that capture silhouettes of nature, a paint-like, tone-on-tone style, and gentle lines."

Lei nani .

OPPOSITE
Fabric swatches
ABOVE AND LEFT
Watercolor artwork and fabrics from Naomi's 2019 spring collection

Naomi working on the art for her
print "Komorebi"

"*Komorebi*—the sunshine that shines
through the leaves—is like rainbow-color
wind or a fragrant breeze. It brings forth
nice feelings, which reminds us of those
days we all surely miss. Lights dance,
and flowers start to sing with delight.
This textile brings out such a calm and
quiet happiness."

Naomi starts her designs by sketching on white paper. She then paints with watercolors or draws with ink. She creates collages of her paintings and drawings and uses color photocopies to experiment with the scale of a motif or pattern, taking into consideration "what is a comfortable rhythm to wear or touch" and continuing to cut and paste until she achieves her final design.

Instincts and feelings guide Naomi from an initial sketch through the design process to a finished textile. She does not compromise on any aspect of her work and will revise a design until it perfectly represents her vision for the piece. Through this process, Naomi remains motivated by "the excitement of the moment of completing the designed textile."

nani IRO prints on different fabrics

Pencil and ink sketches for "Situation" and "Harbe," nani IRO 2019 release

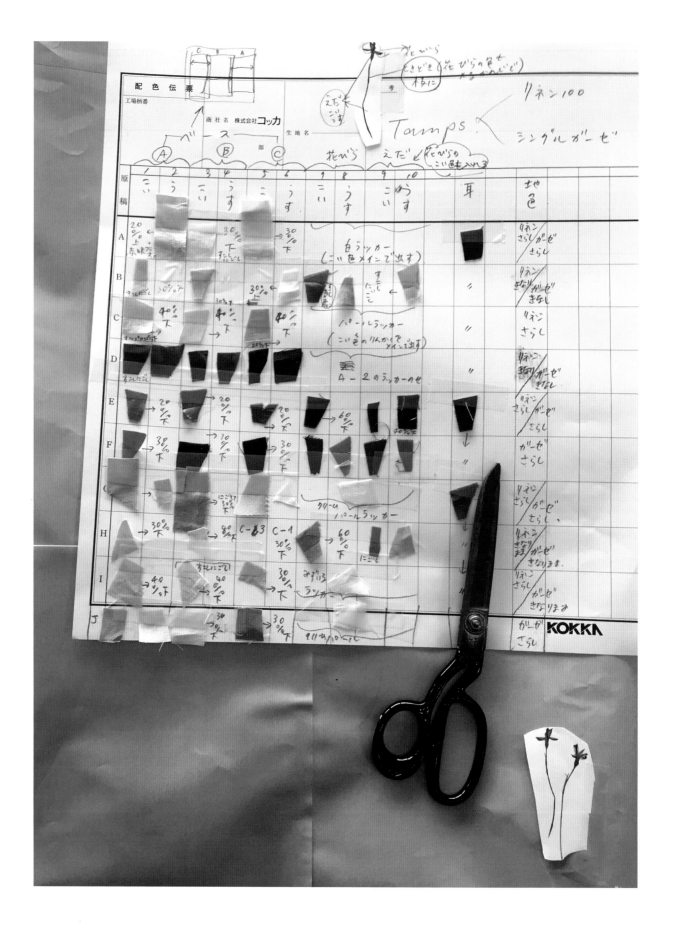

nani IRO cloth may include more than twenty colors in a single design. Naomi carefully chooses each color from a set of cloth color samples: "The only criteria for choosing a color are my fantasy and my imagination." When fabrics are printed, a separate screen must be used to apply each color. At times, colors may appear to shift in value or hue based on proximity to other colors. Naomi works closely with the printing factory to ensure that the colors on the final cloth meet her exact specifications.

Naomi also carefully considers the base fabric for each design, choosing one that reflects the mood or character of the piece and how it will be used for sewing. The texture of the cloth against the skin is another consideration. These substrates include lightweight cotton double gauze or lawn and semi-sheer to medium weights of pure linen, sateen, and jacquard-woven cottons. Naomi also incorporates traditional Japanese techniques such as *enshuku*, or salt shrinking, to create a seersucker-like texture on lightweight fabrics.

Naomi's paintings capture images and impressions of nature and then evolve into textile designs. Each design is suffused with her wonder and joy at nature's ever-changing variety. Naomi thinks of them as poems or letters from her soul, creating a connection with someone in a faraway land through the joy of choosing, making, and giving.

OPPOSITE AND LEFT
Color and fabric swatches illustrating Naomi's complex palettes
ABOVE, RIGHT
Garments made from nani IRO cloth

"My hobby is to have my teatime. I am learning about Chinese tea. This artistic and silent time is important to me. When I draw pictures, I always prepare tea. I will choose tea leaves based on each day's condition, and I will adjust my mind while preparing tea before I start drawing."

Sally Kelly

SALLY KELLY LONDON
LONDON, UNITED KINGDOM

Sally Kelly always knew that she wanted to be a designer and painter. As a child on the Isle of Wight, off the south coast of England, she loved to explore the outdoors and to draw elaborate patterns from her imagination. Sally's doodles blossomed into fantastical landscapes. Her mother, a talented painter who never sold her work, encouraged Sally's creativity and artistic ability. While attending a one-year foundation course at Southampton College of Art, Sally determined that textiles were her passion and accepted a place at Central Saint Martins, in London, where she specialized in printed textile design. Moving from an island of fewer than 150,000 inhabitants to a metropolis of 8 million was "the most exciting thing ever!"

Sally began her career at Liberty London as a temporary sales assistant in the scarf hall. "Everyone who studied textiles wanted to work at Liberty, and if it meant starting on the shop floor, that was fine. We all wanted a Liberty scarf and were lucky to be able to wear whatever we wished in the shop," Sally recalls. She progressed to the role of buyer for the card and Christmas department and traveled to the Philippines, India, and across Europe and the United States to find and develop products. She particularly enjoyed working with small craft makers to develop commercial products with a handmade, unique identity. Sally then moved into product design for the company and developed lifestyle collections using Liberty's iconic fabrics.

TOP, LEFT
Sally Kelly
TOP, RIGHT
Two colorways of "Tresco" print
©Liberty Fabric Ltd
BOTTOM, RIGHT
Limited-edition art print "Arboretum"

"Tresco" ©Liberty Fabric Ltd

TOP
Floral paintings
BOTTOM, LEFT AND RIGHT
Sally in her studio

After her daughter was born, Sally took time off before returning to Liberty as a textile designer. The position was initially temporary, but she stayed on as a senior designer. Liberty London releases two main fashion fabric collections per year, each comprising approximately thirty designs, available for six months. Particularly popular designs, such as Sally's "Tresco" and "Karter," join the likes of William Morris's "Strawberry Thief" in the *Classics* collection, which is always in production.

Liberty collections begin with a concept for the season, developed by the head of the design studio. As many as eight designers work on a project. While a team travels on research trips to collect information and imagery and discuss ideas, everyone brings their own personality to the brief. "This is always a really important part of the creative process. It creates a narrative, the beginning of the story, and provides the designers with the necessary inspiration and drive to create something beautiful. We were always encouraged to be really playful and experimental," Sally explains. She has created designs for Liberty's famous Tana Lawn Cotton, for furnishing fabrics, swimwear, and for signature collaborations, including Kate Moss at Topshop and Manolo Blahnik at Liberty.

"Fornasetti Forest" design created for Liberty's 2016 collection, *The Artist*
© Liberty Fabric Ltd

One of Sally's favorite fabrics is "Earthly Delights," designed with "Floral Earth" and "Winterberry" for Liberty London's *Garden of Temptation* collection. Inspired by the richly decadent depictions of fruit and flowers by Italian Renaissance artist Giuseppe Arcimboldo, Sally rendered each exquisite element individually in oils. "It was a labor of love and an introduction to the utter joy of working with oil paint. It is now my absolute favorite medium." The lush imagery captures the opulence of a Renaissance banquet and features unexpected appearances by bees and beetles, referencing the symbolism of the period's art.

Sally is constantly gathering and recording design inspiration. She snaps photos with her phone at London street markets, junk shops, and high-end department stores; visits art exhibitions; and wanders through miles of museums. In addition, she keeps an extensive archive of photographs taken at some of her favorite gardens, including Sissinghurst Castle Garden and the Tresco Abbey Garden.

OPPOSITE
"Earthly Delights" design for
***Garden of Temptation* from Liberty**
Fabric's Winter 2017 collection
©Liberty Fabric Ltd

ABOVE
"Floral Earth" print in blue colorway
created for *Garden of Temptation*
©Liberty Fabric Ltd

BOTTOM, LEFT
Initial pen-and-ink drawing for
"Milkyway" from Liberty Fabric's
Spring 2017 *Castaway* collection
©Liberty Fabric Ltd

BOTTOM, RIGHT
"Milkyway" print
©Liberty Fabric Ltd

Sally begins developing her designs by collaging her photographs to create beautiful jungles of flowers and plants. She captures ideas by sketching and explores the images with paint, pencils, oil pastels, and inks. Sally either paints whole pictures or creates individual elements of a design before scanning the images and experimenting in Photoshop and Illustrator. For fabric designs, she lays out the repeating pattern and creates colorways on the computer:

Color, to me, is the pure joy that can create absolute magic in a design... Within a collection, the different prints must work harmoniously together but not repeat each other. Different color stories create different moods to appeal to a varied audience. I like to have a classic palette, a neutral palette, and a playful, contemporary one. I spend a lot of time researching color and creating mood boards with photographs, images from magazines, threads, fabrics and ribbons, and Pantone chips...It takes time and patience to tweak the colors...Slight differences in tone can make all the difference.

"Twilight Dancer," a limited-edition print created during the UK lockdown in March 2020. The first edition of this print was given to London's Lewisham Hospital.

Sally has been a freelance designer since 2016 and has a studio at home. She occasionally misses being part of a team, so she arranges frequent chats with other freelancers to share ideas or to visit exhibitions together. "People often ask if it is difficult to stay motivated when you work freelance, but this has never been a problem for me. My work really doesn't feel like a job—it's a passion, and I am never happier than when I have a paintbrush in my hand." Sally challenges herself to try new things so she doesn't slip into a "very comfortable way of working.

ABOVE
Embroidery-embellished print "Prince Paisley"

TOP, RIGHT
"Modern Love" quilt, designed by Kathy Dought, using prints from Sally's 2020 *Solstice* **collection for Windham Fabrics**

BOTTOM, RIGHT
Solstice **prints in "Sunrise Sunset" quilt, made by Tamara Kate**

Sally's love of all things botanical grew into a continuing collaboration with the Royal Botanic Gardens, Kew. She designs packaging for a line of body products sold in their gift shop. She finds inspiration in Kew's collection of more than two hundred thousand prints and drawings of botanical art, some of which date back to the eighteenth century.

This involves marrying illustration with typography within the confines of the shape and scale of the packaging…With fabrics, the design has to repeat and flow beautifully so the repeat lines become invisible. When I design fabric, it is usually very densely covered in detail, and often that is not appropriate on packaging. I have to stop myself from filling every space.

ABOVE
**"Miriam" design, inspired by
Highgrove's Wildflower Meadow**
RIGHT
**Highgrove products using
"Miriam"**
OPPOSITE
**Wildflower Meadow at the
Royal Gardens at Highgrove
© GAP Photos/Highgrove—
A. Butler**

Sally was commissioned by Highgrove, the private residence of Their Royal Highnesses the Prince of Wales and the Duchess of Cornwall, to create designs for use on products sold to benefit their charitable fund. "Miriam," based on the estate's famous Wildflower Meadow, captures the delicate yet vibrant beauty of the organic Royal Garden. The design is named for Dame Miriam Rothschild, who created the meadow's original seed mix of thirty-two species and was a pioneer of sustainable gardening.

"I let myself be inspired by the beauty of the world and try to express it in a way that's true to the spirit of the times."

After leaving Liberty London, Sally began to design collections of quilting cotton and cotton lawn for Windham Fabrics. Bright, bold *Butterfly Dance* was released in 2018 and captures the essence of summer with butterflies, dragonflies, and a meadow bursting with blooms. *Fantasy*, from 2019, was drawn in Sally's "doodle style," the beginnings of which are visible in her childhood sketchbooks. "I've always enjoyed working organically—without a plan, using minimal equipment—and just seeing where the pen takes me." Whimsical story-book flowers, accompanied by a variety of spots and stripes, express elements of light, shade, space, and pattern density. Sally's recent line for Windham, *Solstice*, "celebrates the beautiful botanical bounty of our world and is designed to bombard the senses with a riot of colors and patterns." As she continues to expand her business, Sally Kelly London, she looks forward to each new venture: "As soon as one project is over, I can't wait to move on to the next one!"

OPPOSITE, TOP
Sally painting
OPPOSITE, BOTTOM
"Meadow" print from Sally's 2020 *Solstice* collection for Windham Fabrics
ABOVE
***Fantasy* collection designed for Windham Fabrics in 2019**
RIGHT
Quilt made from Sally's *Fantasy* collection

Cecilia Mok

CECILIA MOK
SYDNEY, AUSTRALIA

Cecilia Mok is an artist, designer, and painter, and a lover of color, storytelling, and wonder. Her surface designs are explorations of rich color palettes, movement and flow, and decorative illustration. Born and raised in Sydney, Australia, Cecilia earned a B.A. in communications and went on to study fashion design at the Sydney Institute of Technology. For her coursework, she was awarded the New South Wales State Medal for Fashion Design and Industry Practices. "I was completely passionate and committed to the study of a broad range of design subjects," she says. "This began my path to surface design." After graduation, Cecilia worked full-time as a graphic designer at a sports-apparel company and studied traditional oil painting at the Julian Ashton Art School at night to earn a degree in fine arts.

Cecilia's job as a graphic designer provided excellent training in Illustrator, which became the basis of her digital surface design. Her "incredibly fulfilling" work as an oil painter allows Cecilia to bring her inspirations to life:

My painting informs my surface designing, and my sense of design and color influences my painting. My art celebrates the natural beauty of this world at the edges of the otherworldly. My paintings are representative of what I see, combined with layers of the subconscious, memories, and storytelling. Landscapes are filled with the memory of a place and the emotions of a day. Portraits often transform into dreamscapes of the subject. A floral still life can blossom into a forest.

TOP
Cecilia Mok
BOTTOM
Brush ink-pen workings and elements for "Phoenix Garden"
OPPOSITE
"Phoenix Garden" in Spring

To Cecilia, patterned textiles are works of art. Her passion for textiles and pattern design was ignited by the philosophy of William Morris and the Arts and Crafts movement: that all homes should be decorated with objects both practical and beautiful. She deeply admires the painting skills of the movement's designers. Cecilia also finds inspiration in imagery from the golden age of illustration that occurred during the late nineteenth and early twentieth centuries, ancient Chinese and Japanese textiles, elaborate European chinoiserie, the work of contemporary picture-book artists, and Australian painters.

She is constantly driven to create and design:

Everything excites me! Seeing an elaborate antique wallpaper, admiring shades of blue in a set of tiles or the bold colors of a contemporary painting [sparks] the idea of a story I want to tell in one scene. When I hear a piece of music, I imagine how I can create that feeling visually. The whole world is vibrating with ideas!

LEFT
Cecilia's studio, with inspirational images, studies, paintings in progress, and uplifting art from her children
ABOVE
Cecilia's oil painting *Sunday on the River*

ABOVE
"Phoenix Garden"
RIGHT
A corner of Cecilia's studio

Inexorably drawn to prints and patterns, Cecilia fills scrapbooks with clippings from fashion and interior-decorating magazines, pieces of wrapping paper, packaging, and fabric scraps. "I love the feeling I get when I see a beautiful pattern…which activates my imagination,… sparks a childhood memory [with] its design or color palette, or simply captures a sense of playfulness and joy." Cecilia describes herself as a fabric hoarder and admits she can't resist buying little samples of fabric to add to her extensive collection. Her stash includes "snippets" she collected as a child when she went to fabric stores with her mother, a talented seamstress who made clothes for herself and for Cecilia and her sisters. "My mum is now making clothes for my kids, using the fabric she kept from when I was little!"

Cecilia loves to be outside with her children: going on a bush walk, swimming at the beach, or flying kites. Together they spend many week-end afternoons at the dining-room table with piles of paper, painting with watercolors or exploring new materials and techniques. "They are very curious about my art making and will follow along, only to produce something far more original and exciting than I could!" Cecilia also teaches at a children's art studio, where she encourages young people "to express their unique personalities, ideas, and their hearts through art making and to cultivate a curiosity and sense of wonder."

Cecilia at home with her family

When Cecilia began to design her own textiles, she developed all of her motifs digitally using Illustrator, which allowed for easy color and scale changes. Over time, she became increasingly interested in the singular texture and quality of hand-drawn and painted lines and the visual depth that watercolor and oil-painted elements add to her designs. Cecilia often creates each element of a design individually by hand, so that they can be digitally assembled and layered.

Cecilia offers her surface designs to customers through several print-on-demand companies, including Spoonflower and Redbubble. Several of Cecilia's designs are also featured on Boba baby carriers. She carefully takes into consideration contrast and clarity of color, weight of line, and the size of painted elements over a range of mediums and end products.

OPPOSITE

"Mid Century Droplets" in Kaleidoscope, "Aquamarina" in Kaleidoscope, "Bauhaus Geo Dreams," and "Daydreaming"

LEFT

Cecilia's oil painting *Branches of the Golden Tree*

ABOVE

Elements painted in gouache for "Underworld Garden"

TOP
**Most of Cecilia's design work is
done at the desk in her studio,
surrounded by inspirational images
and constant music**
BOTTOM
**"Birds and Blooms Chinoiserie"
in Duck Egg**

As a mother of young children and an art teacher, Cecilia sets aside two- to four-hour blocks of time to work on design projects, often between her kids' bedtime and her own. Cecilia and her partner, also a painter, share a studio, "a room with a big window and too many books." While she prioritizes client work and projects with a deadline, Cecilia will create self-imposed deadlines for projects of her own that she finds particularly important or inspiring. At times, Cecilia feels challenged by "finding the right balance between spending enough time on a design so the idea has had time to develop, mature, and be the best version it can and working on it longer than is productive; it's the law of diminishing returns."

Cecilia dreams of having her own line of upholstery fabrics and wallpapers featuring her painted designs. She seeks to combine "traditional techniques with modern production" for designs that become personal expressions of beauty in individual homes.

"In our age of access, we have boundless information about patterns and fabric making from ancient civilizations and different cultures, from traditional techniques to the most contemporary artisans. We are valuing the work of the artisan over the work of the machine."

Hand-painted elements for "Birds and Blooms Chinoiserie" in watercolor and gouache

Heather Moore

SKINNY LAMINX
CAPE TOWN, SOUTH AFRICA

Heather Moore's career in textiles began with access to high-speed Internet and ancient cave paintings.

Born in Johannesburg, South Africa, Heather studied literature and drama, completed a teaching diploma, and then earned an MPhil focused on educational materials and learning. She spent her early career as a writer and illustrator of children's books and comics. Through her job at a comic book company, Heather had early access to the World Wide Web; later she found inspiration in blogs, online tutorials, and Etsy. "It was relatively easy for an untrained person like me to try out textile design just for fun. In the past, work like mine would have been invisible except to friends and neighbors—these days, a person's tryouts and experiments can turn into a business!" Heather, "consumed with jealousy at [the] productiveness" of design practitioners she saw online, started experimenting with Photoshop and a screen-printing kit to combine her intricate cut-paper designs and her love of textiles into a small business.

ABOVE
Heather Moore
OPPOSITE, TOP
Skinny laMinx pillows:
Colour Pop, Graphite, and Lemon
OPPOSITE, BOTTOM LEFT
"Bowls" print in Graphite,
Persimmon, and Lemon Slice
OPPOSITE, BOTTOM RIGHT
"Ilanga" chair with "Flower Fields"
in Penny Black

Heather's style developed as she and her husband, Paul, were setting up a home together in Cape Town. They were drawn to secondhand furniture from the 1950s, '60s, and '70s, which was very affordable at the time. Heather's bold, minimalist patterns incorporate elements of mid-century modern style: "I was looking at what we were getting furniture-wise and other things from that era—textiles and light fittings—and developing a sensibility around that."

The first textiles Heather produced for sale were inspired by ancient cave paintings in the Cederberg Mountains, several hours north of Cape Town. During an escape from the city to write a children's book, she visited the caves with a friend who is an expert in cave art:

> They are an important part of South African heritage, of the Indigenous people known as the San. Cave paintings were very much a part of my childhood but always depicted in a souvenir context, rendered on ashtrays or horrible brown tablecloths, so I'd never paid them any attention. But when I started looking, I could see how incredibly well observed and finely rendered the little animals were, despite rough walls and simple tools. I wanted to show these beautiful paintings to other people, share my new view of them. So that's what I tried to do when I used the cave paintings as motifs in a series of clean, simple, Scandi-style patterns called *Sevilla Rock*.

LEFT
Hand-printed fabrics in Heather's studio
TOP, RIGHT
One of Heather's cut-paper designs
BOTTOM, RIGHT
"Herds" print in Hide Grey
OPPOSITE
Skinny laMinx tablecloth with "Large Pincushion" print

Heather rented a small studio and began screen printing her designs on tea towels. She launched a blog and Etsy shop called Skinny laMinx in honor of her slinky little Siamese cat (whose official name is Monkey). As sales increased, Heather moved to a larger studio and hired professional printers and stitchers. Her first major wholesale order, from California company Heath Ceramics, prompted Heather to quit her job at the comics company in 2009 and turn to designing and running the business full-time. In 2012 Skinny laMinx opened a shop in central Cape Town on Bree Street, a thoroughfare popular with shoppers and foodies.

Heather uses two types of base cloth for Skinny laMinx yardage and products: 100 percent cotton cloth and a 70/30 percent cotton/linen blend. Both are sourced from a large textile mill in King William's Town, Eastern Cape, one of the few remaining mills in South Africa. Heather strives to keep all elements of supply and production for her business as environmentally friendly and local as possible. Her designs are printed at a workshop only twenty minutes from her Bree Street studio, using rotary screen printing and nontoxic water-based inks. The process is mechanized, but "it's still very hands-on. It just doesn't use as many muscles, and there's a lot less waste than [with] other methods."

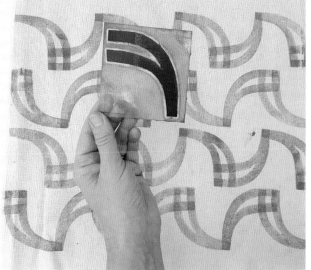

ABOVE
Heather's studio
RIGHT
Creating a pattern
OPPOSITE
Heather in her studio

Skinny laMinx products, such as pillows, aprons, table runners and napkins, tea towels, hats, and several styles of tote bags are cut and sewn in a studio above the shop. "Having an on-site workshop makes us very nimble in the shop, and it makes our customers very happy because it's so easy for us to customize." A cutter and four seamstresses create products in the studio, while nine additional team members manage and coordinate all other aspects of the business. "Although everyone on the team has a specific remit, we are all pretty familiar with all aspects of the business; so we're able to help each other out when needed. It makes for a very cooperative and cohesive workplace, which we all seem to enjoy."

Collaborations have featured Heather's designs on a variety of products, such as wallpaper from Robin Sprong, a stationery collection with Chronicle Books, and a line of mid-century-inspired wooden chairs by Fechters, upholstered with Skinny laMinx canvas.

Skinny laMinx pillows

Heather describes her design flow and the creation of fabric collections as a somewhat mysterious process:

> I always compare it to when you're looking at a star in the sky and you can't really see it; but if you look off to the side, you see it better. I make a lot of stuff all the time. Most of the time I don't know why— I'm doing it just to make things. I have another studio where I can make a mess; it might be cut paper, ink drawings, block printing, or linocutting. I cut things out of magazines. Then I pin it all up, I look at it and pull things together, and a story eventually reveals itself. It's a bit of a sideways approach. I like to catch myself by surprise.

LEFT
A chair in the Skinny laMinx shop, covered with "Roof Garden" fabric in Rio
ABOVE
Skinny laMinx "Roof Garden" fabric in Mumbai

Heather's idea board for
"Sunny Side"

SERIOUSLY,
HAVE A
NICE DAY.

Heather captures inspiration from everyday objects, such as cups and cutlery, shapes and shadows of plants, and architectural elements. She is also inspired by her travels, teaching classes in block printing and pattern design in India and Portugal. A 2019 Skinny laMinx collection featured images of suns after Heather traveled to Switzerland and visited a retrospective show of mid-century modern design icon Alexander Girard. "With all the suns he used, I just found myself drawing suns and noticing suns, and eventually they all kind of came together. I was doing a lot of soul-searching, too, and thinking about what's happening to the world and how everything's going pear-shaped! It's about the value of optimism, too."

When Heather feels pessimistic, she reminds herself of the goals she espouses for herself and Skinny laMinx. The business deals in matters of style and decoration, and she firmly believes that humans need beauty to thrive. But Heather is also keenly aware that for many people, having enough food and money is a far more pressing concern. "Really," she says, "I'm trying to build a resilient business and create a positive work culture."

RIGHT
Skinny laMinx "Sunny Side" tea towels
OPPOSITE
Printing a "Sunny Side" tea towel

Skinny laMinx

"In the past, work like mine would have been invisible except to friends and neighbors—these days, a person's tryouts and experiments can turn into a business!"

Giuseppe A. Ribaudo

GIUCY GIUCE
QUEENS, NEW YORK, USA

Giuseppe Ribaudo's most vivid childhood memories are of fabric. He often accompanied his grandmother, a professional seamstress from Sicily, to fabric stores and recalls the pure joy of "getting to touch the fabrics and feel the fabrics and see the fabrics" as she made selections to clothe her family. Giuseppe learned to sew at a young age but kept his skills in reserve until his early twenties, when he took a costuming class at a community college on Long Island. Fascinated with the potential of a sewing machine, simple notions, and colorful fabric, Giuseppe experimented with garment sewing but never felt the spark of "wanting to create over and over again." He made his first quilt several years later, while studying acting in Seattle. That first quilt, a simple pattern in subdued tones of aqua, burnt orange, and olive drab, was enough to ignite his passion for textiles and the seemingly infinite ways that colors and designs interact.

As his interest in sewing and quilting blossomed, Giuseppe started an Instagram account under the name Giucy Giuce and connected with a global network of quilters and lovers of design. In 2014, Andover Fabrics contacted Giuseppe and asked if he would design a fabric collection.

ABOVE, LEFT
Giuseppe A. Ribaudo
ABOVE, RIGHT
Spectrastatic **prints in Giuseppe's studio**
OPPOSITE
Spectrastatic **by Giucy Giuce**

He presented a very early iteration of his first line, *Quantum*, to the design team at Andover. They wound up hitting it off, but instead of printing the collection, Andover offered him a job as social media coordinator. A year later, he was promoted to multimedia manager. The fabric collection was "put on the back burner" for three years while he created marketing campaigns for Andover's many designers, whose styles range from historical reproduction to the leading edge of modern.

In those three years, I evolved significantly as a quilter and certainly as a designer. I took in all the things that I saw and learned along the way. My style of sewing is what informed my design aesthetic and helped it evolve into…*Quantum* by 2018. I was a quilter before I was a designer, so I approach design very much with an end product in mind. Many of the elements in my collections are mechanical, because I want a very specific end result. I think, *Oh, I would love to do this or that. I wish I had a fabric that could…*

Panels and prints from *Quantum*

Giuseppe's studio

Giucy Giuce designs focus on "high-impact, low effort" prints and panels. His designs often originate in "really wanting an element of a quilt to look particular and complicated without having to work terribly hard to achieve it." Designs that can be used as a whole or divided into tiny subsections, with dots and lines to create texture, are vital to Giuseppe's style of quilting, particularly his foundation paper piecing patterns. "I'll make a four-inch block that has a hundred pieces in it. When the fabric is cut up, it gives so much movement and visual interest." But he also provides quilters who prefer to work with larger pieces myriad options for effortless borders and central medallions.

Giuseppe's designs begin as a list of ideas and quick sketches in a small notebook he carries in his backpack. When a group of ideas feels complete, he starts to engineer the designs with Pilot VBall pens, Sharpies, and sturdy paper.

ABOVE
Giuseppe and a quilt he created from *Quantum*
RIGHT
Giucy's tiny paper piecing

When I drew *Quantum*, I had all of these sketches and ideas and iterations that had been forming for several years. I stayed up until four o'clock in the morning for a week straight and drew everything all at once. Once I found the momentum, I just couldn't stop drawing!... To feel it leaving my body was really, really invigorating. I was wide awake at three o'clock in the morning with the next idea and the next and the next.

Going so far as to draw his own graph paper, Giuseppe creates each design by hand using a ruler and improvised templates, such as the bottoms of mugs and bowls. He takes his completed drawings to the technical studio at Andover Fabrics and works closely with the team there to create perfect repeats and polish the final designs. While sewing his first samples with *Quantum*, Giuseppe noticed marker lines left on his cutting mat from his original drawings. *Oh my god!* he thought. *That's the line from this piece of fabric I'm holding. This is real! It's not just a dream anymore!*

"Interconnection" prints next to marks Giuseppe made on his cutting mat when he first drew the design

Highly engineered Giucy Giuce designs are only one part of the way Giuseppe tells his story with cloth. Color is crucial. Giuseppe favors the "weird in-betweens, deeply saturated hues with pops of bright color—the colors I want to wrap myself in." His spectrum, established with *Quantum* and expanded in subsequent collections, encourages debate: "Is that yellow or green? Purple or gray? The colors transform when they are next to each other."

Not all of Giuseppe's designs spring from his sewing needs. He also includes personal elements:

When my grandfather passed away, my friend Chen sent me a card. It said "Perhaps they are not stars in the sky, but rather openings where the love of our lost ones shines down on us to let us know they are happy." It was the first time that I actually felt OK. "Polaris" was one of the first designs I drew. This star—this little, off-color star—is my grandpa.

"Nucleoid" is actually a reproduction print of sorts. It's based on a fabric my grandma, who's still with us, had in her house when I was growing up. I added the dots, but it had this linework. I have a piece of my grandma and my grandpa in this collection.

LEFT
Quantum
ABOVE
Giuseppe with his first collection, *Quantum*

Not only does Giuseppe design fabric and work in marketing for Andover, he designs quilt patterns and travels to teach his techniques for English and foundation paper piecing. He has released many lines with Andover, including *Redux*, *DECLASSIFIED* (with print names such as "Redacted," "Crop Circles," and "Cipher"), and *Inferno*. His collections have been met with great acclaim, and his ideas show no signs of running out. "I have ideas right now for at least six more collections. Hopefully, I will never have to stop designing fabric because I enjoy the process so much!"

"In the world of modern, the story is told through color— not color more than design, but color before design."

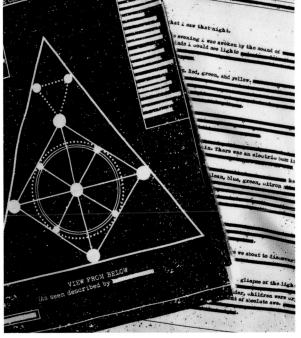

ABOVE
Prints from *DECLASSIFIED* collection
RIGHT
"Redacted" print from *DECLASSIFIED*

Katarina Dragutinović Roccella

KATARINA ROCCELLA
BELGRADE, SERBIA

Katarina Dragutinović Roccella was born in Belgrade, Serbia, to
a family of artists. Her father, a painter, and her mother, a ceramic artist,
provided Katarina and her sister frequent opportunities to design and
create at a young age. Like so many little girls, she dreamed of being
a fashion designer but opted to study graphic design and printing at the
University of Arts in Belgrade. During Katarina's undergraduate and
graduate studies in applied arts and design, she received multiple awards
for drawing and graphic design, including Best Graduating Student.
She employed aquatint and linocut printing techniques in her graphic
designs and created collages from her printing experiments.

In 2001, when she was expecting her first child, Katarina stopped
printing to avoid the acids and chemicals used. At home with her young
daughter, she took the opportunity to learn to sew. She had her mother's
vintage sewing machine, which was in "catastrophic condition," repaired
and taught herself to sew by watching videos and scouring fashion
magazines. She started making twirly skirts for her daughter and designing patterns for fanciful children's garments, which she would sew and
sell in shops around Belgrade and on Etsy under her own label, Like
flowers and butterflies. In the former Yugoslavia, it was difficult to find
textiles that appealed to Katarina's sense of design and style, but unlim-
ited fabric options were available via the Internet.

I was spending so much money at online shops and on Etsy; I [thought]
maybe I should find something that would provide me with money to
spend on fabrics. Then I discovered Spoonflower! Through Spoonflower,
I discovered techniques for repeats, tiles, and designs for textiles. After
a few years, I had a lot of designs, and I made a portfolio.

ABOVE, LEFT
Katarina's "Dear Deer" quilt
ABOVE, RIGHT
Prints designed by Katarina for Blithe
OPPOSITE
Katarina Roccella

Katarina submitted her collection of fabric designs to several U.S.-based companies over several years. The companies replied with "No," "Maybe," or "Your designs are great, but we're looking for something else." Not to be deterred, Katarina submitted her printed portfolio to Pat Bravo at Art Gallery Fabrics when the company began to license work from outside designers. "My first collection was launched in the spring of 2014…It's like a dream come true when you see your designs published on fabric. Every time I have a new collection and see the strike-offs, I am super excited, just like the first time!"

When Katarina designs a collection, she starts with a theme: something that inspires her or a story she wants to tell. She begins by doodling with pen and paper. After the first sketches, she determines which motifs will be the focal prints and then designs blenders to enhance the main prints. "I would like everything to be 'main,'" laughs Katarina. "But the blenders and minimalistic designs are important so that the main prints can stand out." She paints or draws nearly all of her designs by hand instead of using a computer; she prefers an "old-school style," with an organic, slightly imperfect quality to the textures and lines.

"You cannot have anything that is more perfect than nature itself. The texture and the colors! Every time you see a flower, you think, How is this even possible?"

LEFT AND OPPOSITE, TOP
Katarina sketching
OPPOSITE, BOTTOM
Katarina working with the digitized images of her paintings

Katarina's artwork for her "Tropicalia"
print from her *Esoterra* collection,
illustrating how she manipulates
hand-painted elements in Photoshop
to create her final designs
OPPOSITE
Katarina drawing

Choosing color is the second part of Katarina's process. When approximately half the designs in a collection are completed, she scans them into Photoshop. Unlike Illustrator, Photoshop allows her to maintain the hand-drawn quality of her lines. Katarina often chooses an initial palette that she changes as she creates the second colorway.

Katarina's design work is frequently influenced by the modern art scene. "There are times when you see something that creates an impact on your work. Maybe sometimes you are not conscious of the influences that remain inside you." Also deeply influential is the Bauhaus school and movement. Her collection *AvantGarde* pays homage to the Bauhaus style of design, as well as to the work of Sonia Delaunay, a painter and pioneer of abstract art who was also a textile and fashion designer.

"Nature is one of the biggest inspirations, because you cannot have anything that is more perfect than nature itself. The texture and the colors! Every time you see a flower, you think, *How is this even possible?* You can never imitate nature perfectly."

"There are times when you see something that creates an impact on your work. Maybe sometimes you are not conscious of the influences that remain inside you."

LEFT
Katarina's collection *Grid*
TOP, RIGHT
"Megapixel" quilt, designed by Katarina and made with prints from her collection *Grid*
BOTTOM, RIGHT
Pen-and-ink drawing of a lace doily

Katarina draws and designs every day, not only for fabric. She is working toward a Ph.D. in design, incorporating painting, graphic design, and textiles. Katarina's 2018 collection, *Grid*, focuses on squares and pixels. The "simple square" is a theme of her dissertation, exhibitions, and installations for her postgraduate work. "What was the analogic form of the square? Now it is a pixel translated onto monitors. I am exploring the connections and communication between what was before and what is coming next." Some of Katarina's textile installations are interactive; she provides visitors with large baskets of fabric squares and a design wall: "You can arrange everything just like what I had in my head, but you are going to have your own moment of creativity to make something different. Maybe something better."

Katarina has released more than fifteen collections with Art Gallery Fabrics. Her personal style is always evident, but her diverse inspirations are expressed through various design genres. "I have these moments when I need to tell something different, even though I am not sure that everybody is going to like it…It's important to have the courage to try something different and something new and something that is really meaningful for you."

Quilt made with prints from *Grid*

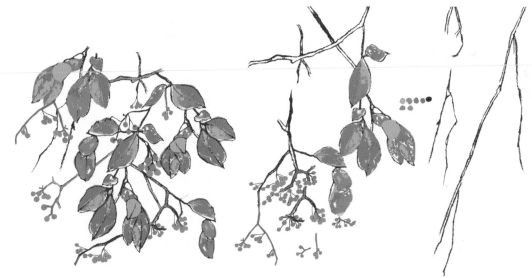

Ruby Star Society

Melody Miller, Alexia Marcelle Abegg, Kimberly Kight, Rashida Coleman-Hale, and Sarah Watts are Ruby Star Society. They are artists and designers who describe themselves as "friends, sisters, creators, trendsetters, stargazers, hell-raisers, and modern-day makers." The women met over several years at different Quilt Markets, the quilting industry's semi-annual trade show. Their friendship and deep respect for one another as designers grew, and they decided to pool their talent.

For their first working meeting, in 2013, the five designers met in a hotel in Los Angeles to collaborate on their designs; they spent an intense week learning how to work together.

"We holed up in a hotel for a week with printers and computers. It was a big question as to how the workflow would go, but everyone was really comfortable about stepping up and doing things and sharing roles and brainstorming together," Alexia remembers.

"I think that fell into place immediately the first time that we all worked together," Sarah adds.

"We brought all this art for our first collection release, and we were laying it all out in this meeting room, all over the floor," Alexia says.

"We had a white bedsheet on the floor because the carpet was so ugly and awful," Rashida laughs.

ABOVE
Ruby Star Society

"We were in a hotel conference room, and we were sleep-deprived, and we had all these snacks everywhere. We immediately started playing around with each other's artwork, and it was awesome because it felt like college again, and we all miss that," says Sarah. "You know—pin your artwork up on the board and critique it with each other. I loved that so much. I think that was part of what made me fall in love with the group right away. It felt right immediately!"

"We walked away from that experience with an intense connection with each other. We just had this chemistry," says Alexia.

ABOVE
Prints from Ruby Star Society's collaborative quilting collection *Darlings*, **used in the "King's Dash" quilt by Satterwhite Quilts**

RIGHT
Prints from Ruby Star Society's collaborative quilting collection *Darlings*

That first week defined how they would work and grow together. Since then, as their lives have changed and their families grown, the friends have spent less time "holed up together" but no less time communicating and collaborating. "We're always texting, e-mailing, and sharing images," Sarah says.

Each of the designers has a background in the quilting, sewing, or fabric-design world. Inspired to form a collective of fabric designers, Melody Miller pulled the group together and in 2013 founded Cotton+Steel, a modern division of RJR Fabrics. For five years, the designers released many collaborative and individual lines under the Cotton+Steel brand, then parted ways with RJR in 2018.

Unwilling to leave the world of fabric design, Melody, Alexia, Kim, Rashida, and Sarah resolved to "regroup and rise." To guide themselves through that time of turmoil and transition, they relied on their individual and collective strength and their determination to share their

Alexia, Melody, Rashida, Sarah, and Kim at an arcade in Los Angeles, taking a break during one of their first work sessions

creativity. Less than six months after leaving Cotton+Steel, the team became Ruby Star Society, a division of Moda Fabrics + Supplies. Their new incarnation "is a fabric brand and sisterhood rooted in deep connection, supportive collaboration, and, more than anything, the notion that a good idea is worth fighting for."

Ruby Star Society launched its brand in 2018 and its first fabric collections in 2019. The team has released individual collections and blenders from each designer as well as several collaborative efforts. One line, *Darlings*, includes two of each designer's favorite prints from their time designing as a group for Cotton+Steel, but presented in three new colorways. All the group's fabrics can be mixed, matched, and coordinated with current and future collections.

LEFT
Strike-offs from Ruby Star Society's first release
ABOVE
Alexia, Melody, Kim, Rashida, Sarah, and Devon Iott working together at QuiltCon

Each designer develops her own concepts for her individual lines and works independently but always relies on the other designers for feedback and help. The team uses an online platform to upload and share their ideas for a collection. Each member can see the others' collections coming together and offer comments. The designers have weekly video calls to discuss their work.

"Sometimes we'll just get stuck. If one of us is trying to hammer something out and has an idea for a print and it's stuck in the mud, we have this whole team of artists to help us get through those moments," Alexia says.

For their collaborative collections, they agree on a central idea or theme. Each designer submits ideas for prints, and then the group works together to give feedback and select which prints will make up the collection.

"We look at what is going to serve the collection best," Alexia explains. "'How does this all work together?' instead of 'I've gotta make sure I get my art in this one.'"

The "Mod Diamonds" quilt pattern from Pen + Paper Patterns, featuring *Aviary*, a Ruby Star Society collaborative quilting collection

Melody, founder and creative director, and Devon Iott, brand manager, work together in Ruby Star's Atlanta Studio. Melody says:

> My job is at the end. Everybody pulls their collection together based on group feedback and finessing it on their own. I print everything out, and there's just something that happens when you can see it on paper. It shows where the holes are or where things still need connecting… At that point, I give a lot of individual feedback, send lots of photos, and just try to do that last level of tightening everything up and getting it ready for production.

Melody also works closely with the guest designers who collaborate with Ruby Star Society. Sasha Ignatiadou, a designer from Germany, shared her talents and love of nature, art, and female beauty in her line *Airflow*, launched in late 2019.

"Hana" in Jade by Rashida from Ruby Star Society's collaborative collection *Aviary*

"Moda is trusting me to lead this group with my creative vision for Ruby Star Society. We do all of this continually in collaboration with Moda," Melody says, "and it's fantastic for us."

The team worked closely with Moda to create a new, slightly lighter-weight cotton substrate for Ruby Star Society prints. "It's really soft and versatile; it's great for making quilts but also great for garment making."

Designing for additional substrates is a collaborative effort for the team. For example, while exploring options for their first release of cotton/linen canvas, they worked together to select a style or theme for the collection. Then each started submitting designs, and they created a group of prints to choose from. Some Ruby Star Society prints are also available in lightweight cotton lawn and rayon.

Through Moda, Ruby Star Society has been able to expand the range of products it offers to makers. Sarah Watts has released multiple 108-inch-wide panels featuring her fantastical animals, along with pillow-sized blocks and large-scale prints that can be used as quilt tops, backing fabric, or anything a maker can envision. Also available are "Guaranteed Delightful" goods featuring prints from each designer. These include ironing board covers, double-sided cotton throws, tote bags, socks, and sewing tins.

ABOVE
Canvas 2019, one of Ruby Star
Society's collaborative collections

RIGHT
The Crescent Tote pattern from
Noodlehead, made from Alexia's
"River Rocks" canvas in Navy

ABOVE
**"Lindley" lawn print by Kimberly
in Persimmon**

RIGHT
**The Tiffany bag from Sallie Tomato,
made from Melody's *Canvas 2019* print
"Peaches" in Caramel**

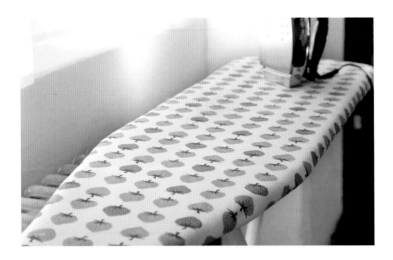

TOP
Kimberly's "Strawberry" ironing board cover

LEFT
The Ruby Star Society double-sided tote

RIGHT
Finished projects from Sarah's "Magic Unicorn" panel

OPPOSITE
Melody working at the Ruby Star Society studio

Ruby Star Society's mission is to create collaboratively, honoring and building on the strength and long legacy of women in the arts of quilting and making. The designers state on their website:

> The history of quilting is rich and beautiful: generations of women stitching together fabrics woven with memories, dreams, and secrets. But it's also a story of companionship, connection between artists, and the powerful things that happen when you work hard to keep a skill alive and celebrate both all that it meant in the past and what it creates for the future.

Melody, Rashida, Sarah, Kimberly, and Alexia are a "sisterhood of empowered women" who dedicate themselves to helping people exceed their own creative expectations. They believe in "bringing [their] best talents together to create something greater than any of us could have created on our own." They share their collective strength, gained through life's struggles and joys, and their deep personal connections with other "big dreamers."

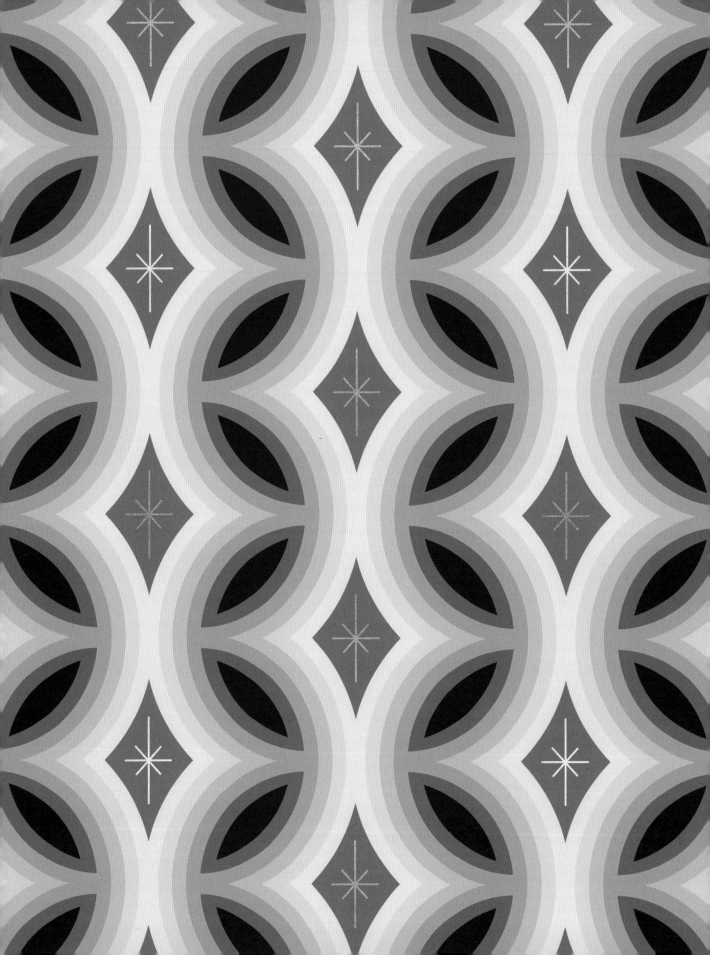

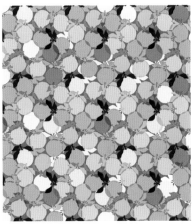

Melody Miller

RUBY STAR SOCIETY
ATLANTA, GEORGIA, USA

A lifelong artist, Melody Miller decided to trade in her corporate job for the world of design after the birth of her second child. "We had recently moved, and I couldn't find any curtains I liked," she recalls. Undaunted by the fact that she didn't know how to sew, Melody designed curtains and hired someone else to sew them—until her seamstress suddenly disappeared.

"I emergency-found someone on Craigslist to give me a sewing lesson and ended up hiring her to just sew the curtains…While I was practicing and trying to get better at curtains, I started sewing these little animal shapes just to do something more interesting," she says. Melody turned the animal shapes into tooth cushions and put them on her Etsy shop. *DailyCandy* picked them up, and they sold like hotcakes. "I got a herniated disk from all the sewing that I was doing!"

"I decided I needed to rethink my strategy—not be a one-person sweatshop," Melody explains. Having a baby, she grew interested in baby bedding and "really began looking at fabric for the first time." She fell in love with Japanese prints from Kokka, but, unclear on the rules about using a designer's fabric in manufacturing, Melody decided to design her own.

OPPOSITE
Melody's "Rattan" print in Bright Blue
ABOVE, LEFT
Melody Miller
ABOVE, RIGHT
Melody's print "Clementine" in Bright Blue

She first discovered Quilt Market through Kim Kight's blog, *True Up*. "It was one of the first on my radar," she says. "I went to Market in 2009 with a portfolio [and] met a few manufacturers." Kokka offered her a contract.

Melody generally draws her designs directly in Photoshop or Procreate. "Usually I give myself a little talk about how I'm going to go with something subdued and sophisticated," she says. "And then it's always the wildest, craziest, most complicated of everyone. I don't know why! Somehow I need to complete a two-thousand-piece puzzle every time I make a piece of art: lots of color, lots of layers, lots of textures."

One of Melody's biggest challenges stems from being on a delivery schedule that calls for major collections at least twice a year. "Sometimes it feels like your brain isn't ready even though the calendar is," she says.

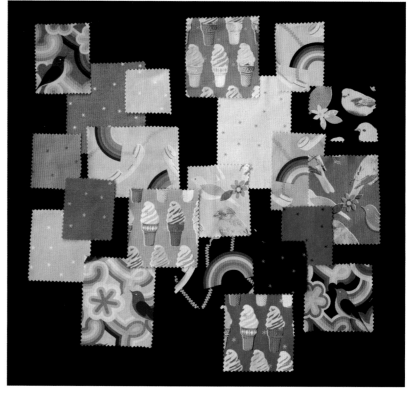

ABOVE
Melody's "Good Morning" print in Red
RIGHT
***Social* and *Spark*, Melody's first collections for Ruby Star Society**

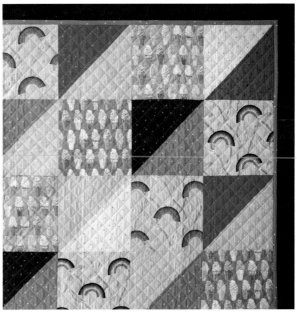

TOP
Melody looking through strike-offs from her collections *Social* **and** *Spark*

BOTTOM, LEFT
The Rose dress from Olive Ann Designs, made from Melody's "Ice Cream" print in Pink

BOTTOM, RIGHT
Melody's "Rainbow Ice Cream" quilt pattern made from her *Social* **and** *Spark* **collections**

Something that really helped was my personal one-hundred-day challenge in 2019. Initially, I created the challenge to draw a flower every day as a way to better learn Procreate without putting any pressure on myself to do great work or incorporate the drawings into my fabric designs. I just wanted to build a new skill and give myself plenty of time for progress. After about a month, I started to see a style develop. Over time, I was able to find my voice in this new medium, and suddenly I had lots of new art for my fabric designs.

As creative director for Ruby Star Society, Melody thrives on collaborating and working directly with individual artists on contemporary fabric design. "They submit their work, and then I see an opportunity to adjust or tighten something up or pull it together a little more. I love that part of the process where you just see this magic happen, where the collection really gets polished at the end."

Having founded Cotton+Steel in 2013 and then Ruby Star Society in 2018, Melody has observed a natural progression in her self-perception: "I noticed that I'm starting to think of myself as an independent artist again, instead of my identity being completely about the brand. That's been a nice development."

Procreate drawings from Melody's personal one-hundred-day project in 2019. These florals became the basis of her Spring 2020 collection, *Rise*

Alexia Marcelle Abegg

RUBY STAR SOCIETY
NASHVILLE, TENNESSEE, USA

Alexia Marcelle Abegg grew up in Northern California. Her mother, a seamstress and designer, and her father, a musician and painter, encouraged their daughter's innate creativity. Their gifts to her were most often art supplies or experiences. Growing up surrounded by creativity and art influenced Alexia's path toward fabric design; the journey has included photography, custom tailoring, and wardrobe design for films.

In 2011, Alexia partnered with her mother, Michelle, to launch Green Bee Patterns, based in an old hosiery factory in Nashville. Together they create modern patterns for clothing, quilts, and bags. Green Bee provided Alexia an entrée to Quilt Market trade shows, where she met Melody, Rashida, Kim, and Sarah. Her skills in art and illustration, sewing, and pattern design made fabric design a natural next step.

Alexia's bohemian upbringing instilled in her the belief that everyone should seek the joy in life: "There's so much darkness everywhere. I think I'm always trying to find that happiness in my artwork or share the idea of lifting people up—lifting up women especially— and honoring the women who have made an impact in my life."

OPPOSITE
Alexia's "Swatch" quilt pattern, made from her collection *Alma*
ABOVE, LEFT
Alexia Marcelle Abegg
ABOVE, RIGHT
Alexia's print "Butterflies" in Indigo

"I love textiles and the way that art changes once it is printed on fabric," Alexia says. "It's fascinating how things look on paper compared to cloth. I am creating a design that will be printed on a flat surface, and it needs to be beautiful in that state, but it also must look even more interesting and beautiful when the flat shape is given dimension and form through the act of sewing."

Alexia is a woman of many creative pursuits. Rashida describes her as "a literal sewing machine! She paints, does pottery, stamp making, screen printing, knitting. You name it! She can do it like a pro and make it look easy!"

Designing fabric with the Ruby Star Society sisterhood leaves time for individual pursuits, and Alexia has developed her own line of ceramics. Her hand-thrown mugs, vases, bowls, and more are decorated with designs familiar to followers of her fabric; they express a range of forms and glazing techniques. The process of designing imagery for ceramics is similar to that of fabric design: flat illustrations applied to a three-dimensional object take on a new life, creating a unified whole that is independent of the original image.

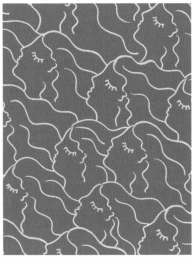

LEFT
Alexia's print "She" in Earth
ABOVE
Alma and *Add It Up*, **Alexia's first collections for Ruby Star Society**

Alexia's passion for creating something new by gathering various elements was the theme of her first release with Ruby Star Society. *Alma* honors the ties of family, friendships, community and the women who share their strength with those around them. Alexia's design "She" is a reminder of the resilience women have as individuals and as part of a community. "It's not easy to be a human. Life is full of ups and downs, and we can build each other up if we choose to. My aesthetic is very much informed by always seeking things that remind me of happiness in some way. I want people to feel warm and happy when they see my work."

When creating *Warp & Weft*, part of Ruby Star Society's third release, Alexia drew on her experience designing wovens for childrenswear. In a shift away from drawing, painting, and block printing, she focused on geometric elements and color in designing the entirely woven line.

Alexia delights not only in collaborating with her sister designers, but also in connecting and collaborating with a global community of makers who use her fabric to create something entirely new.

ABOVE
Alexia's *Warp & Weft* collection of woven designs
RIGHT
Alexia's woven design "Mountain" in Warm Red, for *Warp & Weft*

Rashida Coleman-Hale

RUBY STAR SOCIETY
BAY AREA, CALIFORNIA, USA

A peek into designer Rashida Coleman-Hale's work space opens up a world of color. Gifts from friends and family, treasures collected on her travels around the world, and a huge collection of Japanese design books fill the space. Heavily influenced by Japanese objects and language as well as color in general, Rashida has translated her love of sewing and illustration into a successful business as a Ruby Star Society designer.

Surrounding herself with beauty inspires her sophisticated designs, which Sarah Watts describes as having a "really interesting way of being conceptual and clever…There's just something about the way that she simplifies an idea into these beautiful shapes and the way that things interlock with each other that's really special."

Rashida keeps and constantly refers to a notebook of ideas. Most of her work "comes from random doodles." She sketches on paper or in Procreate and then pulls in elements of her drawings to compose surface-pattern designs in Illustrator. "I literally have a file of all these ideas that I've come up with," she says.

OPPOSITE
The "Party Hat" quilt pattern from Ruby Star Society, made from Rashida's collections *Pop!* and *Zip!*
TOP, LEFT
Rashida Coleman-Hale
TOP, RIGHT
Rashida's print "Starfetti" in Blue Raspberry, part of her *Pop!* collection
BOTTOM
Rashida's "Pop Off" print in Cream Soda, part of her *Pop!* collection

"I'm a daydreamer," Rashida explains. "As an only child, I spent a lot of time entertaining myself...That's definitely where my work comes from."

Rashida's multicultural childhood involved living for several years and spending every summer in Japan, where her mother was a fashion model. After studying fashion design at the Fashion Institute of Technology, in New York City, Rashida worked as a freelance graphic designer. When her first child arrived in 2006, her love of stitching was renewed and she began the blog *I Heart Linen*.

The transition was natural, since Rashida hails from a long line of makers. Her mother and grandmother were avid sewers, and her grandfather, who taught her most of what she knows about sewing, was a tailor in the West Indies. "When my grandfather passed away, my grandmother gave me all of his scissors, and I still use them to this day," she says. "I think about him often when I sew."

Rashida's collection *Stellar*

Rashida's first book, *I Love Patchwork*, was published in 2009, and her second book, *Zakka Style*, followed in 2011. She created collections with Timeless Treasures and Cloud9 Fabrics and was a founding designer of Cotton+Steel before designing for Ruby Star Society.

For Rashida, now a mother of four, positive energy comes from face-to-face interactions at places like QuiltCon. She loves engaging with the people who buy the fabric and make things. "I love their excitement for the work and what they're doing with it. They bring projects to show us and tell us some really heartfelt stories of something that happened because of one of our prints. That's invigorating and inspiring."

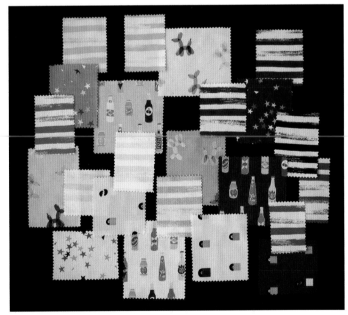

TOP, LEFT
"Moon Hills" in Pale Peach
BOTTOM, LEFT
The "Expanding Stars" quilt pattern by Emily Dennis of Quilty Love, created from Rashida's collection *Pop!*
RIGHT
***Pop!* and *Zip!*, Rashida's first releases with Ruby Star Society**

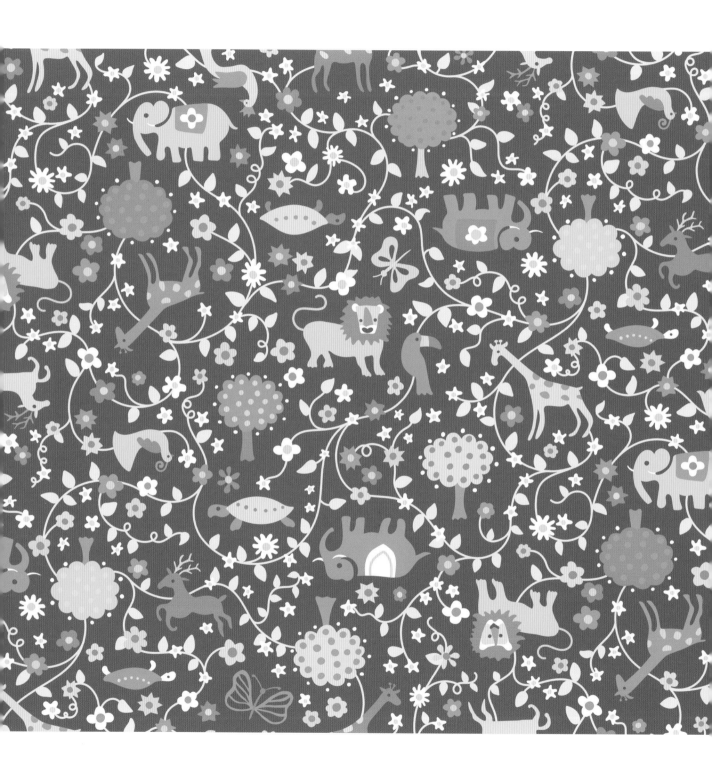

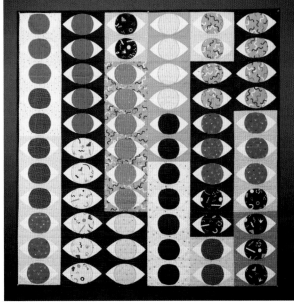

Kimberly Kight

RUBY STAR SOCIETY
AUSTIN, TEXAS, USA

A lifelong "art dabbler," Kimberly Kight began sewing as a hobby. She soon found that she was more interested in fabric than sewing. "When I started," recounts Kimberly, "there wasn't a lot of fabric that spoke to me." She scoured thrift stores and online sources and began to collect vintage fabrics. Kim saw an untapped niche in the quilting fabric industry and immediately wanted to print her own fabric, but she found that there were few resources for fabric printing. Her research inspired her to start a blog about fabric. Until 2011, *True Up* provided fabric lovers with a "global fabric fix," featuring interviews with designers, collection previews, links, and a "swatch of the day." Always faithful to its tagline, "all fabric, all the time," *True Up* soon became an industry favorite. Melody Miller cites Kimberly's blog as her "gateway to the industry" when she first began to explore fabric design.

In 2011, Kimberly released *A Field Guide to Fabric Design*. Still in print ten years later, her book offers straightforward instructions on color theory, creating designs and repeat patterns using traditional and digital techniques, and multiple methods for creating fabric from those designs.

OPPOSITE
"Liana" in Saddle by Kimberly
ABOVE, LEFT
Kimberly Kight
ABOVE, RIGHT
Kimberly's quilt pattern "Staring Contest" for Ruby Star Society, featuring her *Anagram* and *Grid* collections

The inspiration for many of Kimberly's designs comes from vintage fabrics. "I've collected a lot of fabric over the past twenty years. There are pieces in my collection that I love and think should live again, and I try to build a story from those. Sometimes it's a mash-up of different prints. Sometimes it's literally just a jumping-off point; I start with one print but change it so much that it becomes something totally different."

With her vintage fabric in front of her, Kimberly traces directly from a swatch into Procreate or an Adobe app on her iPad, depending on the look she wants. Antique typography is also a source of inspiration. She draws in black-and-white and adds color last. Sarah Watts describes her Ruby Star colleague's color sensibility as "Retro Airstream…like fun seventies wallpaper and couches." Kimberly notes that she often finds herself in a "blue, pink, and rust world" but is also drawn to bright reds and yellows.

Working full-time as a speech therapist, Kimberly finds that one of the most challenging aspects of fabric design is finding the time to do it. With the support of Ruby Star Society and Moda, however, Kimberly can focus on her "happy place." She explains, "I love just working and getting in the zone, when the hours go by designing and moving things around and recoloring. I just love it!"

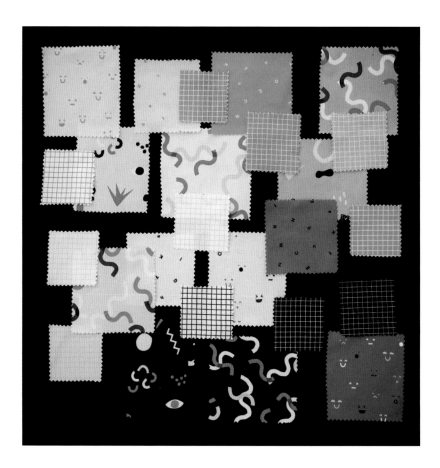

Anagram and *Grid*, Kimberly's
first collections for Ruby Star Society

Grid, Kimberly's basics collection for
Ruby Star Society's first release

The "Kalle Shirtdress" from Closet
Case Patterns, made from Kimberly's print
"Novelty Shapes," sewn by Devon Iott

Sarah Watts

RUBY STAR SOCIETY
DALLAS, GEORGIA, USA

Animated, quirky Atlanta-area designer Sarah Watts says that if fabrics were music, hers would be "gothic, indie, dubstep." She expresses her unique style with ink-work in a limited color palette, depicting mythical and real animals. Sarah's natural-world inspiration shows in every piece she designs, whether for Ruby Star Society or Craftedmoon, the business she runs with her husband, Scott Cormack.

Constraining her artwork to limited colors and subject matter helps Sarah focus her active mind on providing just enough detail to bring her funky design ideas to life. "Whenever I'm coloring my artwork, I tend to only use three or four colors. It's mostly because my brain is filled with stuff all the time, so I have to simplify everything else in my life," she explains. "I can sit here and come up with twenty different business ideas or twenty different collections…but I've got to just home in and focus. Part of my style and sensibility has come from a place of just needing to organize everything, so that I can enjoy life with a little more clarity."

OPPOSITE
Ruby Star Society's "Bullseye" quilt pattern, designed by Alexia, featuring Sarah's collections *Crescent* **and** *Brushed*
TOP, LEFT
Sarah Watts
TOP, RIGHT
Crescent **and** *Brushed*, **Sarah's first collections for Ruby Star Society**
BOTTOM, RIGHT
Detail from Sarah's panel print for her collection *Crescent*

Sarah has worked hard to streamline her process as well. She begins with black-and-white ink work, which she then scans and colors in Photoshop. More recently, she's discovered Procreate on her iPad, which allows her to work in color, she says, "in a way that I can't with paint or watercolor…It's magical! I'm learning a new creative process that I feel like I've been missing out on for a long time."

The simplicity Sarah espouses in her artwork carries over into her day-to-day life. "I like a lot of simplicity, as far as the way that I dress and the things that I consume. I'm very bland and methodical with certain things so that I can focus on my family more and let my artwork run wild."

Sarah's artwork has been running wild her entire life. In childhood, she was always creating things: playhouses, drawings, holiday windows. "I grew up in a family that had a lot of troubles," she says. Art was a welcome, steady passion to get through the hard times. As Sarah's entrepreneurial spirit soared in high school, creative work became more than a source of solace; it became a way to help her family financially. Encouraged by her early successes, she graduated from Ringling College of Art and Design with a degree in illustration. "I've always sworn to myself: No matter what, I am going to make a living doing what I am passionate about, and nobody's going to stop me. And I picked art."

The Molly bag from Sallie Tomato, made from Sarah's "Chrysalis" print in Dark Teal

ABOVE
**Sarah's "Mother" print in Slate
Gray from her collection *Tiger Fly***
RIGHT
**Sarah's "Chrysalis" border print
in Shell**

ABOVE
Sarah working on her art
RIGHT
**Craftedmoon art print with
a paper cut**

As her career evolved from book illustration and clothing design to fabric design, Sarah became part of the founding group behind Cotton+Steel. When they decided to leave RJR Fabrics and become Ruby Star Society—"a supportive girl squad that you can bounce ideas off of"—part of the agreement was that each of them would have enough time to pursue her own interests. Sarah and her husband, Scott Cormack, took the opportunity to launch Craftedmoon, which features Sarah's artwork and inspirational quotes on various gift items. As Sarah and Scott describe it, "Craftedmoon is the first stationery and gift brand to create artwork that specifically honors the crafty homebody."

Of her drive to make a living selling her artwork, Sarah says, "I am just obsessed and determined to make a living from this. It's my addiction. I really love seeing how far I can push the envelope with it."

Craftedmoon art print

Destiny Seymour

INDIGO ARROWS
WINNIPEG, MANITOBA, CANADA

Destiny Seymour is Anishinaabe, First Nation. Her textiles give new life to the designs found on the pottery shards and bone tools of her ancestors. Frustrated by the lack of textiles that related to her people's Indigenous identity, Destiny, an interior designer, began to create her own textiles. "It's taking those patterns and giving them a modern twist, so that we see ourselves in these interiors and in these spaces," she says.

Destiny has always been interested in architecture and design. As a child, she would sit in the back of her mother's hair salon and create dollhouses—many dollhouses. She didn't play with dolls; she just made houses for them and gave them to her friends. Destiny earned a master's degree in interior design from the University of Manitoba faculty of architecture. She worked at a local architecture firm for more than ten years designing interiors for public spaces, including schools and daycare centers. Destiny found it very difficult to find designs and finishes that represented the Indigenous people of Manitoba: "If you go to Vancouver or Seattle—the West Coast—there are a lot of fabrics and blankets and things like that. Then also Navajo and Southwestern designs. There are patterns that we use, but they don't represent us here." Destiny decided that she would create textiles that reflect the designs of her heritage.

OPPOSITE
"Niish" print by Destiny,
of Indigo Arrows
TOP LEFT
Destiny Seymour
TOP, RIGHT
"Bezhig" pillows
BOTTOM, RIGHT
"Ishkoday" long lumbar pillows

"A woman brought me pottery shards that she collected near my family home. It's about two hours north of Winnipeg. I was so shocked! There's a piece that looks just like one of the patterns that I designed. It gave me goosebumps, because it's from where my family's ancestors are from."

ABOVE
Indigo Arrows screen-printed fabrics drying and ready to be sewn into finished home goods
RIGHT
Anishinaabe pottery shard

Destiny took evening classes in silkscreen printing, but, she explains, she didn't receive "formal training, like a fine arts degree. It was a lot of trial and error. Taking those lessons really helped, starting from the basics and learning how to actually do pattern making." Two years later, in 2014, Destiny launched Indigo Arrows.

"In Manitoba, the Anishinaabe have a very rich pottery history because we have large clay deposits in our rivers. There are over three million pottery shards that the Manitoba Museum is cataloging. I've been visiting the museum because that's where our collections are held right now, still in the museum," Destiny says. The designs from these shards, ranging in age from four hundred to three thousand years old, form the basis of her designs.

Destiny's process begins with careful study of actual artifacts, sometimes drawing, sometimes taking pictures. Then she sketches with pencil and india ink on paper before making screens in her studio. Using those screens, Destiny creates different pattern variations by printing and overprinting, shifting her screens, and layering printed vellum.

Destiny's sketches, based on designs from her ancestors' pottery shards

Destiny with one of her "Bezhig"
long lumbar pillows

Destiny also uses block printing as a way of developing her surface designs. While she figures out a pattern, she doesn't get caught up in creating a perfect finished product. She begins by carving blocks and experimenting with them: "What helped me get to where I am now was to just get messy and make, make, make. There are a lot of patterns that I didn't like. It can be scary, but at the same time, it's so rewarding and fun when you just let go." She transfers her block-printed images to screens and further refines the designs:

> I pin the prints all over my house…When I print on fabrics, I put those up, too. When my two girls were little, I noticed that they would also make little sketches, and they would tape them below, close to the floor. It takes me a few weeks to really come up with something. I want to make sure that the story of where that pattern came from is shared in a respectful way. I feel a responsibility. I don't want to *just* make something.

Destiny anticipates that soon pieces such as bedding and large textiles for interiors will be digitally printed in Canada, while smaller Indigo Arrows products—pillows, tea towels, and napkins—will continue to be screen printed by hand. When screen printing, Destiny often uses her own custom-mixed copper metallic ink: "I really like the way it looks. It works well with the history, the patterns themselves, and the story behind them."

Indigo Arrows lumbar pillows

TOP
Destiny screen printing with her custom-mixed copper ink

BOTTOM, LEFT
Destiny's hand-mixed copper ink is both beautiful and culturally significant

BOTTOM, RIGHT
Screen-printed linen tea towels

Destiny realizes the potential of using her ancestral designs as a teaching tool and a way to share her culture. Each Indigo Arrows print is named in Anishinaabemowin, the Ojibwe language. "Non-Indigenous people are speaking our language without even knowing that they're speaking it," says Destiny.

Whenever I attend a pop-up market, the general population in Winnipeg are so shocked that this history is there, that we have a rich pottery collection and history within Manitoba. They don't have to be Indigenous to appreciate the history behind these pieces…They're buying something that's good quality but also has a story to it.

Indigo Arrows screen print

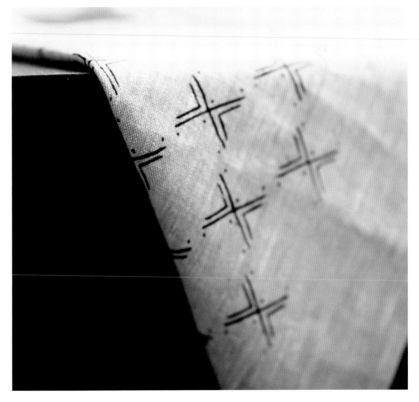

ABOVE, LEFT AND RIGHT
**Indigo Arrows "Niish" print, screen
printed on linen**
RIGHT
"Niswi" pattern on a linen napkin

Destiny describes herself as "fifty-fifty textile designer and interior designer." In addition to Indigo Arrows, she works in a studio called Woven Collaborative. A partnership with another Indigenous designer, the studio focuses on creating collaboration within architecture and design projects. They work closely with their clients, most of whom are Indigenous, to ensure that their project goals are met. "I find that a lot of First Nation clients have felt that they haven't been listened to in the past. Things have been designed for them without their consent. If it's a large project, then I work with either the main consultant, the primary architect, or the design-builder. I make sure my clients' needs are met." Destiny hopes to merge Indigo Arrows and Woven Collaborative to further assist clients with "finding identity within interiors, being able to see [themselves] in that interior and feel welcome…It means something when you know that this pattern comes from your people, from your land…So you're celebrating your culture, and you're sharing it, too."

ABOVE
Indigo Arrows
OPPOSITE
Destiny at sunset on the prairie

Mili Suleman

KUFRI
DALLAS, TEXAS, USA

Mili Suleman was born in Mumbai, India, grew up in Oman, and moved to the United States at eighteen to study liberal arts and graphic design in Dallas, Texas. After working for ten years with an agency as a professional designer, Mili sought a change. "I started to lose interest with graphic design because it was coming too easily to me; it wasn't really a challenge anymore. I wanted something more tangible… something more complex," she explains.

Mili's family had an apartment in Mumbai where she spent school vacations, but she had never deeply explored her native country. Having made the decision to leave the world of professional graphic design, Mili traveled to India and immersed herself in the culture and environment: "I took two exploration trips, one with my dad, one with my mom. I explored different types of crafts just to see what would speak out to me. I love going to the source of where things are made. I like traveling off the beaten path, so I think I naturally gravitated towards interior villages."

OPPOSITE
Weaving supplies at the KUFRI studio
ABOVE, LEFT
Mili Suleman
ABOVE, RIGHT
"Cusco Stripe" napkins

ABOVE
Yarn supplies at the KUFRI studio

RIGHT
Woven samples in the KUFRI studio

KUFRI's woven textiles are produced in the southern Indian states of Andhra Pradesh, Kerala, and Tamil Nadu. Mili acknowledges the challenges of establishing working relationships in remote villages, some requiring four hours and three modes of transportation to travel to the nearest city:

> There was a lot of trial and error in the beginning…There can be communication issues and problems with deadlines and pricing. But I've chosen my village units carefully and have been loyal to them and vice versa for several years now. They understand my commitment and are interested in growing their business with KUFRI.

Mili has tried weaving, but her role remains that of designer. She notes that designing woven fabric is vastly different from designing for print. Woven cloth is designed on a grid that represents the intersections of the warp and weft. "There was a big learning curve. There are so many restrictions! I was coming from a graphic-design practice, where you could do pretty much anything you wanted in Illustrator." Mili spent time traveling to many different villages and learning the art of weaving. "But sometimes when I would design something, it wouldn't get woven that way."

Mili's mood board in the KUFRI studio

In 2019, Mili launched KUFRI's flagship Dallas showroom, featuring sample interior decor made from the cloth that has been produced in India. The showroom also includes a studio space where an in-house woven textiles designer works with Mili. "What I design, she brings to life…We collaborate and make changes while it's still on the loom." The time savings are immense. Mili no longer has to send her designs to India and wait for samples to be made and returned to her before making changes or going ahead with production. "I send my designs with thread references, colors, cuttings, handwritten notes, and notes from the computer…Now we are able to send a real woven sample, too, which is amazing."

ABOVE
KUFRI woven fabrics
RIGHT
KUFRI's line of woven textiles in the Dallas showroom

Mili's designs are inspired by her travels. She looks to a variety of sources to create the mood for a collection: "I gather colors, take pictures, and collect books and ephemera that inspire me. It's loosely put together…It's very organic, and I allow myself to be experimental." Mili loves using photography as part of her recording process. She sketches with a variety of black pens, using different nib and point sizes, and does all of her coloring in Illustrator.

While visiting New Mexico, Mili was deeply inspired by the architecture and beauty of the landscape. She returned to Dallas and used the architectural forms she had seen to design a line of block-printed textiles, which are also produced by hand in India, but in a small artisan workshop in a major city. Mili sends her designs, created from sketches and paintings uploaded to Illustrator, to the block printers. They carve wooden blocks by hand, using simple tools, then create strike-offs from Mili's color specifications. After the strike-offs are approved, the workshop prints the full collection on handwoven cloth made by KUFRI's weavers.

Mili's work celebrates the natural qualities of handwoven cloth. Slubs, bars, and slight irregularities are considered flaws in mass-produced cloth but add life and authenticity to KUFRI cloth. All of the cotton, linen, and silk yarns are manufactured in India, and more than half of Mili's designs include handspun yarn.

BELOW, LEFT
Table linens
BELOW, RIGHT
Woven textiles designer at the KUFRI studio in Dallas

"My mission is to help preserve handloom weaving, to provide employment to women and aging weavers, and promote a conscious, beautiful life at home through KUFRI products."

ABOVE
Artisan weaver
RIGHT
Block printer printing "Roar" design
OPPOSITE
Close-up of block print design "Roar"

216

ABOVE, LEFT
**Exposing the resist-
dyed yarn**
ABOVE, RIGHT
Dyeing yarn for ikat designs
LEFT
**Pillows made from "Rex"
in Blush**
OPPOSITE
KUFRI's showroom in Dallas

Each region in India has its own style of weaving; in India, weavers learn their craft based on traditional designs created for the domestic market. "My aesthetic is different," says Mili. "I like to see what we can do with this process but still keep it fresh and modern. A lot of times the weavers will look at my designs, and they say, 'This is so simple. Are you sure you are going to be able to sell this?' I say, 'Trust me. This is what my clients want.'" One weaving village that works with Mili has particular skill in a style of woven design known as ikat. Yarns are dyed prior to weaving with a resist technique that involves tightly wrapping the yarn in bundles according to a specific pattern. When the yarns are dyed, the bindings prevent the dye from penetrating, and the wrapped portions remain a different color. The finished fabric shows color blocks with soft edges.

When the finished cloth arrives in Dallas, another part of the process begins. Mili and her team design samples and products for showrooms around the country where KUFRI textiles are offered as yardage to interior designers and architects. All of the samples, as well as pillows and table linens, are made by small businesses in Dallas. Mili has also forged manufacturing relationships with local artisans to develop furniture, ceramics, and wallpaper to complement KURFI's fabrics. She strives to keep her global business as local as possible by working only with small artisan businesses at home and abroad.

ABOVE
**Mili Suleman with one of
the weavers**
OPPOSITE
**Block-printed design
"Potishead" by KUFRI**

Through KUFRI, Mili seeks to preserve the craft of handloom weaving. As aging weavers retire and younger generations choose not to take up the trade, the future of the craft is threatened. The availability of inexpensive, mass-produced textiles further imperils the traditional industry. In most of the villages where Mili's cloth is woven, the weavers are quite elderly; another weaving group is made up entirely of women who are divorced or widowed and generally have no other means of support.

It's really important to keep working in these villages; the number of weavers is reducing every year because they age out. All of the kids generally know weaving; it's just that some of them choose not to be in the business or do the craft. But my hope is that if we keep doing interesting, creative work that challenges them and keeps the orders coming, it will encourage the children to stay in the family business.

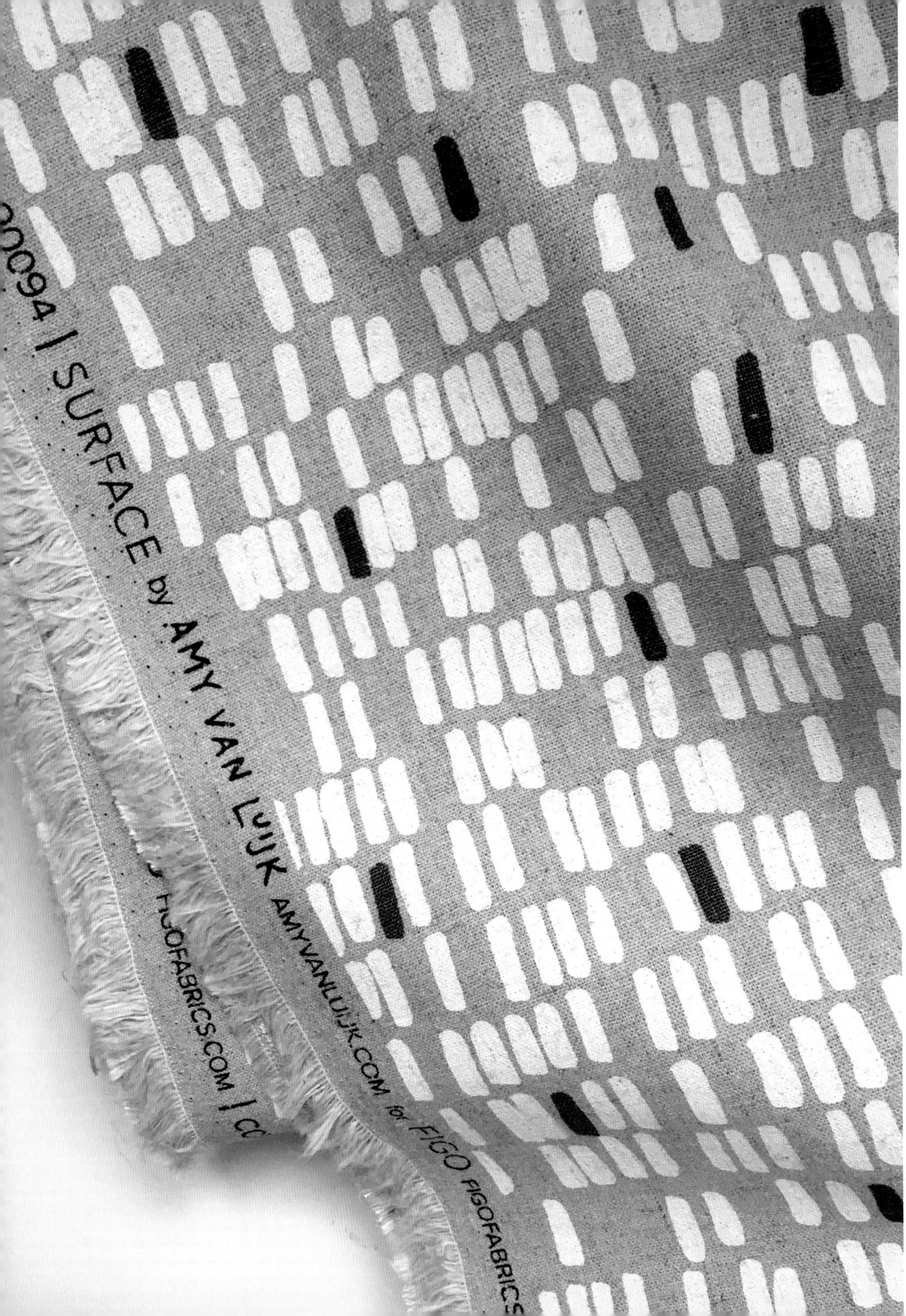
00094 | SURFACE by AMY VAN LUIJK
AMYVANLUIJK.COM for FIGO FIGOFABRICS
FIGOFABRICS.COM |

Amy van Luijk

WELLINGTON, NEW ZEALAND

Amy van Luijk has always designed and made things. Growing up in Christchurch, New Zealand, she sewed by hand until she was six years old, when her mother relented and let her use the sewing machine. Her passion for making led her to study textile design in Wellington on New Zealand's North Island. "I actually produced a kind of fashion collection," Amy says. "The theme was 'wrapping,' and I did things with lots and lots of layers. Prints, layers of organza, everything printed with different colors and then cut through to reveal the layers below."

After graduation, Amy immediately moved to London and worked at several commercial print studios: "I inserted myself straight into it. I rung up some studios and asked, 'Can I intern?' In hindsight, it was quite a brave thing to do." The London design scene was far removed from Amy's concept- and art-based degree program. "That leap into commercial design was a big step, to suddenly realize that I needed to make lots of prints and sell them. I couldn't labor over a single print for a week," she explains. Her work primarily focused on interiors and designs for children; the designs produced in the commercial studios where Amy worked were offered for sale at international trade shows or sold directly to business owners for their collections.

OPPOSITE
Print on a linen/cotton blend from *Surface*
ABOVE, LEFT
Prints on a linen/cotton blend from *Surface*, Amy's first collection with Figo
ABOVE, RIGHT
Amy van Luijk

"I quite like to work with accidents—things that happen spontaneously— and to capture all those little moments. Often the best bit of work will be in the corner of a page, really small."

Following her time in London, Amy returned to New Zealand and continued her design work. She created stationery products and gift wrap with teNeues Publishing and illustrations for books and magazines, including *Martha Stewart Living* and *Real Simple*. Her work appears in the children's television show *Riddle + Squizz*. Amy also designed bedding and coordinates for the Land of Nod, now Crate&Kids. Her playful, often deceptively simple motifs resonate with both children and adults. "I quite like to work with accidents—things that happen spontaneously—and to capture all those little moments. Often the best bit of work will be in the corner of a page, really small. It's all about shape and line and movement, kind of a tension between control and spontaneity."

Amy's favorite medium is collage. She loves colored paper, and she loves cutting things up. She admits, with a smile, that she has drawers and drawers of paper—a collection she has been building since she began to work with collage. "My most charming work is always from little scraps of paper or just bits on my desk. That's how I pick all my palettes. Sometimes there's a little ripped-up bit, sort of just lying there, and that's my new palette." Amy also uses paint, pencils, pastels, and ink to capture her ideas. She loves to use crayons and Chinagraph pencils to create thick, imperfect lines. She often photocopies her drawings and cuts them up, scans them, and rearranges them on the computer. Amy says she would like to be "quicker in a digital sense" and put available technologies to more use when designing, but she always goes back to paper and glue.

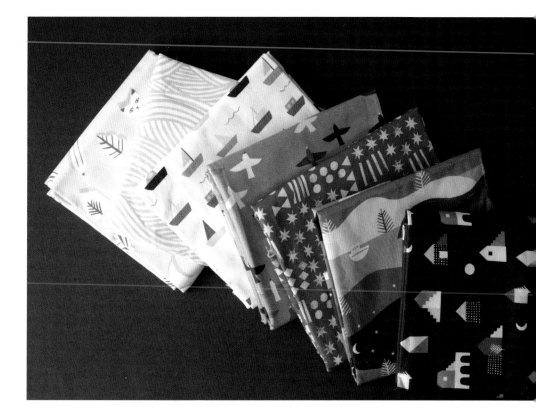

OPPOSITE, TOP
"Fruit" on White collage
OPPOSITE, BOTTOM
Some of Amy's artwork
RIGHT
Prints from *Moonlit Voyage*

Amy loves to find inspiration in new places. She has visited
Japan several times, frequently as an extended stopover while traveling
to or from the UK, and spent almost three weeks on a recent trip:

> I just needed to open my eyes again. When I'm living somewhere,
> even a place as beautiful as New Zealand, my eyes don't see things
> anymore when I see the same things over and over. When I go overseas
> or travel to a new city, I see everything. I see the rubbish on the street,
> the signs, the color combinations—all the little things. I really needed
> an injection of inspiration.

Amy's sources range from everyday objects, like the scissors and
pencils on her desk, to ikebana, the Japanese art of arranging flowers
according to strict rules. She admits to having kept a library book
on the subject for more than a year. "There's a lot of Japanese design
that really inspires my work. There's something about the simplicity
of it and about capturing the spontaneous, natural things that happen
in a composition, things that aren't centered, things that happen
accidentally."

Amy also finds inspiration in ceramics: "All the different forms
and all the different textures and all the different patterns on the
forms." She not only admires pottery, but she also makes her own.
She loves to translate her pen-and-ink drawings from paper to round,
three-dimensional objects and see them in a new form. The same
applies to her designs rendered on textiles. The drape of fabric and the
texture of the substrate interact with the imagery and give Amy new
ideas, and she often uses screen printing as part of her design process
and exploration.

OPPOSITE
**"Still Life" screen printed
on linen**
RIGHT
"Still Life" screen print
OVERLEAF
Amy's studio

When designing, Amy creates full collections of prints. She starts with one or two patterns, often the most intricate, and adds prints within the same color palette. She presents the designs as a collection but says that they are not always purchased as a unit. "People move stuff around. I present them all together, but because they work for so many different applications, they can be used separately as well." Typically, Amy does not design for a specific product:

> When I'm in the designing zone, I just make what comes into my head. Or maybe I've made something and it turns into something else, and then the next step just reveals itself. I tend to go into making phases that last for a couple of days or a week. I just do lots and lots of drawings, and it's afterwards that I look at the drawings and paintings I've made and think of what they would apply to. Sometimes when I think of designing for a specific application, it freezes me a little bit.

ABOVE
Amy looking through her artwork
RIGHT
Working with crayons
OPPOSITE
Stamping

In 2017, Figo contacted Amy after seeing her work on Instagram. The team assembled a collection of Amy's designs, and *Surface* was released in 2018. Printed in Japan on an unbleached 45/55 percent cotton/linen blend, the designs feature smooth waves, curves, and organic lines that show Amy's talent for capturing movement and natural variation. Her collection *Moonlit Voyage* uses cut-paper shapes to create whimsical landscapes.

Amy works in a studio above two art galleries in Wellington. She shares the space with seven designers who work in different fields, including graphic design, typography, and comic-book arts. She enjoys the camaraderie of other artists during the day but also enjoys working at night when her colleagues have gone home. She turns the music up and prepares her screen-printing equipment. "I have a really good time. I make a big mess and then get it tidied up before they come back the next day."

While she dreams of one day having her own line of simple designs on linen, printed locally and sold in New Zealand, Amy loves what she is doing now. She looks forward to continuing to design fabric, creating more collections, and traveling the world to find new inspiration.

ABOVE AND OPPOSITE
Prints from *Surface*

Yumi Yoshimoto

YUMI YOSHIMOTO
NISHIKATSURA-CHO, YAMANASHI, JAPAN

Yumi Yoshimoto always dreamed of being an artist. She studied printing and oil painting in conjunction with her textile design work at Tokyo Zokei University. While pursuing her graduate degree, she entered a design competition sponsored by the Japanese textile firm Kokka. This contest, called Inspiration, takes place every other year to encourage new talent and is the only printed textile design prize in Japan. Yumi was awarded the Jury Special Award for the 2013 competition.

As a student, she launched the label YUMI YOSHIMOTO and created a fashion collection based on "the fun of everyday life" as a theme. In collaboration with a textile factory, she printed her interpretations of life scenes as patterns on cloth and created clothing styles to emphasize various aspects of the printed designs. After completing her master's degree in 2015, she began to work with Kokka to create a collection of textile designs.

OPPOSITE
"River Side" in Pink, a KESHIKI series 3 print from Kokka x YUMI YOSHIMOTO
ABOVE, LEFT
"Office Street" in Cream, a KESHIKI series 3 print from Kokka x YUMI YOSHIMOTO
ABOVE, RIGHT
Yumi Yoshimoto

Yumi's line KESHIKI was launched by Kokka in June 2016. The word *keshiki* translates as "landscape," "scene," or "scenery." Kokka describes the collection as "fabric that decorates ordinary living like a landscape painting." Yumi's designs distill everyday sights such as the sky, mountains, city scenes, and seascapes to their abstract essence with vibrant, hand-drawn lines and textures. KESHIKI is printed on lightweight cotton fabric and a textured, medium-weight cotton/linen blend. Yumi's second KESHIKI line for Kokka was released in 2018, and she plans to release a new collection every other year.

Under her YUMI YOSHIMOTO label, Yumi collaborates with fashion and lifestyle brands to create fabric designs for their products. She worked with Bigi Co. brand Adieu Tristesse on a line of printed fabric for spring fashion designs with vintage French styling. Her designs are featured on umbrellas by Estää, stools from Youbi Studio, Fujie Textile curtains, and silk scarves from Muto.

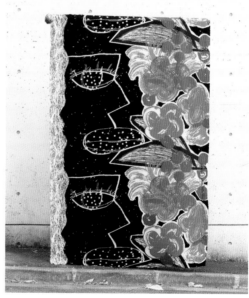

ABOVE, LEFT
"Keep the Sun" print in Green and Orange
ABOVE, RIGHT
"The Woman and Bouquet" print in Black
OPPOSITE, TOP
YUMI YOSHIMOTO shirt made from "Keep the Sun"
OPPOSITE, BOTTOM
YUMI YOSHIMOTO shirt made from "The Woman and Bouquet"

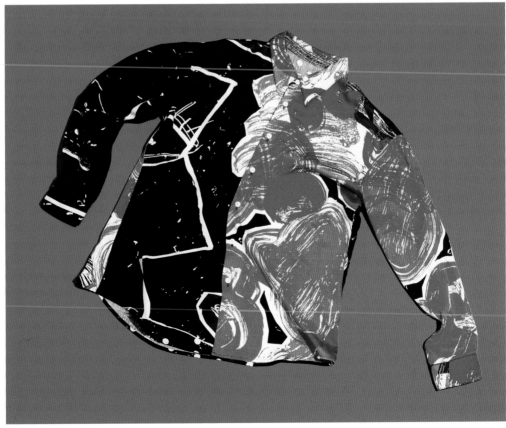

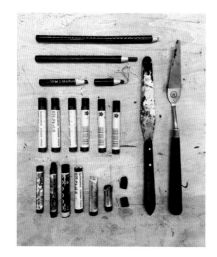

TOP, LEFT
**Tools and supplies Yumi uses
for her artwork**
TOP, RIGHT
**Yumi's home workroom,
decorated with postcards and
souvenirs from her travels**
BOTTOM
Sketching patterns

Yumi takes into consideration how her prints will be used on a finished product: whether the image will be used as a whole, as in the case of scarves, or cut to create garments. Her second collection for Kokka includes both large-scale and smaller-scale prints, to provide fabric that can be used for projects of any size.

When she is creating designs, Yumi first draws a rough sketch, which she edits and polishes on the computer. She often draws her final designs onto a strong transparent film, intended for architectural drawings. She spreads crayons, Cray-Pas, or ink all over the sheet and creates a highly textured pattern with a palette knife, chopsticks, or a spoon. These etched and incised textures capture a movement and momentum that are part of the final design. Yumi admits that deciding on colors is her least favorite part of the design process:

> Therefore, I try picking as many color options as possible. My motto is not to stick to one color, but to prioritize a combination or hue for the whole impression. I love the harmony of individual colors [coming together to create] a unique impression.

Yumi's designs reflect her observations of daily life. She wants to "create textiles that bring outdoor landscapes into fashion and living spaces." She also loves modern art and runway-fashion collections.

KESHIKI series 3 prints from Kokka x YUMI YOSHIMOTO

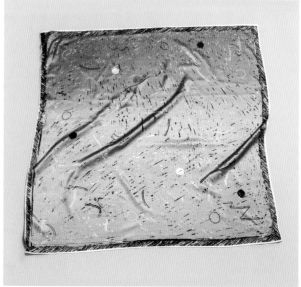

**YUMI YOSHIMOTO scarves
inspired by the view out Yumi's
studio window**
TOP, LEFT
"Moon Makes Big Shadow"
TOP, RIGHT
"Sunset Sky"
BOTTOM, LEFT
"Perfect Laundry Day"
BOTTOM, RIGHT
"Spring City"

Screen printing by hand
produces deep, vivid colors

Yumi is very grateful to her mentors, who introduced her to the "charm of textile arts." Masayoshi Ohashi is an expert in dyeing techniques and color design, and Reiko Sudo is a textile designer and cofounder of Nuno. She is also honored to have worked with Masaru Suzuki, a textile designer best known for his bold, playful compositions inspired by nature, plants, and animals; and with fashion designer Hiroyuki Seike, who established his brand Seike in 1993 and designed and directed Issey Miyake's *Permanente* clothing line.

Yumi teaches textile design part-time at Tokyo Zokei University, where she has joined her mentors as part of the faculty. When she is not teaching or designing in her studio, she loves to play with her young son. She continues to create fabric designs based on the concept of "adding spice and humor to life."

"I try picking as many color options as possible. My motto is not to stick to one color, but to prioritize a combination or hue for the whole impression."

"Office Street" in Blue, a KESHIKI series 3 print from Kokka x YUMI YOSHIMOTO

ABOVE, LEFT AND RIGHT
**"Minato" in Red, a KESHIKI series 3 print
from Kokka x YUMI YOSHIMOTO**

BELOW AND RIGHT
**"Office Street" in Cream, a KESHIKI series 3
print from Kokka x YUMI YOSHIMOTO**

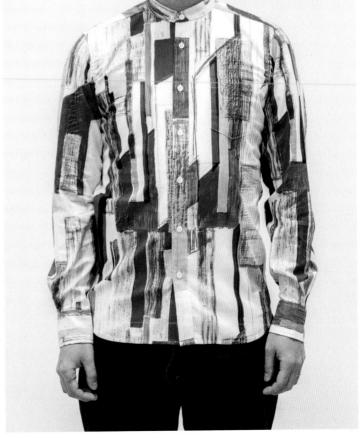

"Minato" in Green, a KESHIKI series 3
print from Kokka x YUMI YOSHIMOTO
"Asa No Yama" in Green, a KESHIKI series 3
print from Kokka x YUMI YOSHIMOTO

Holli Zollinger

MOAB, UTAH, USA

As a child, on a farm in northern Utah, Holli Zollinger thought about fabric while falling asleep at night; those calming thoughts foreshadowed her destiny in design. After high school, she attended several semesters at a local university, then opted to follow her passions away from traditional higher education. She traveled to Asia, Europe, and Central America, savoring the "alchemical experience" of exploration and inspiration. She lived nomadically throughout the American West during her twenties and thirties and recently settled in the small town of Moab in southeastern Utah.

Holli has been a visual artist since her early twenties; she expanded into fabric and surface design in 2008 when she met a vendor at a local farmers market who was selling products made with custom-printed fabrics. Intrigued by the accessibility of designing fabric through print-on-demand start-ups like Spoonflower, Holli taught herself to use Photoshop and Illustrator to create textile designs. "Those first few years were very magical as I set out to find my own style and teach myself the basics of the business."

ABOVE, LEFT
Artwork for Holli's print "Olive Bloom"
ABOVE, RIGHT
Holli Zollinger
OPPOSITE, TOP
"Olive Bloom" and "Boho Tile Marine"
OPPOSITE, BOTTOM
Prints by Holli: "Sun Tile Marsala Dark," "Bebe Meadow," and "Boheme Butterfly Marine"

(Left to right): "Bird of Paradise Dark,"
"Herbal Study," "Floral Study Dark,"
"Junglia Charcoal"

Artwork for "Adobo Multi Desert"

Holli started designing with Spoonflower shortly after the company launched in 2008 and has grown along with it. Her online portfolio contains more than 2,700 design and colorway options that can be printed on twenty styles of fabric or on a wide range of home goods through Spoonflower's sister company, Roostery. Holli's designs are also available on hundreds of items produced through other print-on-demand companies, including Deny Designs and Society6. Deny Designs has opened a larger customer base for Holli through well-established companies such as Nordstrom, Urban Outfitters, and Wayfair. Her work has also been featured on HGTV, in *Better Homes and Gardens*, and on Apartment Therapy. "My portfolio of fabrics on Spoonflower was the main reason I got other gigs in the design industry," Holli explains. "Now I license my designs for products all over the world." She feels especially lucky to have forged relationships with Boba and "mompreneur" businesses Alice + Ames and Dwell & Slumber.

At times, Holli has considered designing for commercial fabric companies but appreciates the freedom Spoonflower offers. "My appetite for designing can't be contained to a few collections a year." In addition to the flexibility offered by print-on-demand platforms, Holli praises Spoonflower's commitment to sustainability and its environmentally friendly approach to printing. Spoonflower's digital printing process uses substantially less water than the more traditional screen-printing process still employed by many fabric companies. The company also works to reduce the use of toxic inks and unsustainable materials by sourcing from carefully selected suppliers.

(Top to bottom): "Bebe Meadow,"
"Junglia Charcoal," "Adobo Multi Desert,"
"Boheme Butterfly Marine"

The search for inspiration is a daily motivation for Holli. She "jump-starts [her] creative juices" by visiting social media sites or Pinterest. "I used to collect magazines and cut out what inspired me and create these quirky little design books," she describes. "When Pinterest came around, I literally threw my hands in the air and praised the sky… So much easier!" Holli is continually seeking new trends and movements to keep her designs and aesthetics current: "I am constantly refining my tastes. In the beginning, I had a lot of unharnessed energy and simply watched what came out. Mostly I still do that…But now I think about how my designs might be received in the marketplace, too."

Holli almost always begins with a simple sketch. "I think my favorite medium has always been the pencil. I love the feel and contact and intimacy in this beginning stage." Recently, her process has evolved to include sketching on her iPad Pro. Her drawings go directly from the iPad to Illustrator without requiring Holli to scan or manipulate the images. Once all elements of a design are in Illustrator, she builds the repeat and decides whether to add texture using Photoshop.

LEFT
Holli drawing
ABOVE
**Holli's prints on a linen/
cotton-blend fabric**
OPPOSITE
"Playa Geo Star" print

While assembling the design, Holli records potential color combinations and ideas for future reference. She adds color—her favorite part of the process—only when the mechanics of a design are complete:

I *do* love the time it takes to apply hundreds of color options, but it can be overwhelming, too. It's often in this phase that I have to step away from the computer and take a walk or go out to the garden and return with a fresh eye. I find it fascinating how each color contributes to the overall feel of the design and how I can change it significantly with another set of colors.

"Ultimately, all of my design work is built on the idea that creativity is life, and my life is about being creative."

Holli thinks a great deal about how colors are traditionally used to create a visual experience, primary colors in particular. She seeks to move away from clichéd combinations and to test boundaries by creating new and unusual yet captivating color relationships. "I like to think I started designing with a 'candy wrapper' color mentality and progressed to appreciate more subtle and natural hues," Holli says.

She designs from her eco-friendly straw-bale home: "I worked really hard to create a beautiful and calming home atmosphere so that my ideas are manifested seamlessly. I have a hard time creating in any other environment." Her work often spreads from her tiny desk to the coffee table and across the kitchen counter; she recently converted an old bus to create additional studio space.

Holli spends anywhere from four to sixteen hours a day sketching, designing, answering e-mail, and scouring the Internet for new trends. She tries to incorporate movement and gardening into her process "to keep things fresh." Although she recognizes the need to relax and combat potential burnout, Holli acknowledges that "for someone who is used to being busy, it's hard to slow down and be OK with it." She spends her free time with her son, Ren, exploring and enjoying the outdoors, hiking, biking, swimming, or rafting. "I just want to keep creating! I don't think there's an end to the amount of inspiration one can receive."

ABOVE
Artwork for "Protea Neutral"
RIGHT AND OPPOSITE
Holli's studio in a converted bus

Acknowledgments

We are deeply grateful to all of the designers in *Modern Fabric*. They gave generously of their time to answer our questions and share their stories with us in person, via video calls, and in writing. They provided us with an exquisite array of images to illustrate their lives and talents.

We also thank all of the people who helped us in so many ways in putting together this book: designers' assistants and staff, photographers, friends who helped to translate emails and interviews—the list goes on and on, and we are grateful to every one of you.

We thank our editors, Jan Hartman and Sara Stemen, for guiding us through all aspects of this project. We thank the publishers, Princeton Architectural Press, for their interest in this subject.

Abby: I thank my husband, Geoff; my children, Noah and Claire; my parents and sister; my extended family; my friends; and my staff at the shop. You all provided so much support and encouragement for me, and I deeply appreciate it.

Amelia: I thank my parents, for instilling determination and perseverance, and Michele Levesque and Michael Rossney, for letting me use a corner of their restaurant as a writing space and for unconditional friendship. I am also deeply grateful for my village of amazing women, who have supported me and my daughter, Lucy, throughout this project. Also, love and many thanks to Lucy for her patience and good humor as we navigate life together.

OPPOSITE

Color spectrum of basics from Ruby Star Society's first release

Designers

Bari J. Ackerman
Bari J. Designs
barijdesigns.com
@barij

Stacie Bloomfield
Gingiber
gingiber.com
@gingiber
Studio and/or store open
to the public:
The Workshop
1503 Carley Road
Springdale, Arkansas

Pat Bravo
Art Gallery Fabrics
patbravo.com
@patbravodesign

Erin Dollar
Cotton & Flax
cottonandflax.com
@cottonandflax
Studio and/or Store open
to the public:
Cotton and Flax
3180 Adams Avenue
San Diego, California

Kaffe Fassett
Kaffe Fassett Studio
kaffefassett.com
@kaffefassettstudio

Erin Flett
erinflett.com
@erinflett
Studio and/or store open
to the public:
Erin Flett Studio + Shop
2 Main Street
Gorham, Maine

Alison Glass
alisonglass.com
@alisonglass

Jen Hewett
jenhewett.com
@jenhewett

Lara Cameron and
Caitlin Klooger
Ink & Spindle
inkandspindle.com
@inkandspindle_
Studio and/or store open
to the public:
SH1.32, Level One
Sacred Heart Building
Abbotsford Convent
1 St Heliers Street
Abbotsford, Victoria
Australia

Naomi Ito
nani Iro
naniiro.jp
@atelier_to_nani_iro
Studio and/or store open
to the public:
ATELIER to nani IRO 1-12-28
Kotobukikaikan, 2F
Kyomachibori, Nishi-ku
Osaka City, Japan

Sally Kelly
sallykellylondon.com
@sallykellylondon
@sallykellycraftfabrics

Cecilia Mok
ceciliamok.net
@ceciliamok_
@ceciliamokart

Heather Moore
Skinny laMinx
skinnylaminx.com
@skinnylaminx
Studio and/or store open
to the public:
Skinny laMinx
201 Bree Street
Cape Town, Western Cape
South Africa

Giuseppe Ribaudo
Giucy Giuce
@giucy_giuce

Katarina Dragutinović Roccella
likeflowersandbutterflies.com
@katarinaroccella

Ruby Star Society
rubystarsociety.com
@rubystarsociety

Melody Miller
@missmelodymiller

Alexia Marcelle Abegg
alexiamarcelleabegg.com
@alexiamarcelleabegg

Rashida Coleman-Hale
rashidacolemanhale.com
@rashida_coleman_hale

Kimberly Kight
kight.kim.com
@kmelkight

Sarah Watts
Craftedmoon
craftedmoon.com
@wattsalot
@craftedmoon

Destiny Seymour
Indigo Arrows
indigoarrows.ca
@indigo_arrows

Mili Suleman
KUFRI
KufriLifeFabrics.com
@kufrilife
*Studio and/or store open
to the public:*
KUFRI
1152 Mississippi Ave
Dallas, Texas

Amy van Luijk
amyvanluijk.com
@amyvanluijk

Yumi Yoshimoto
YUMI YOSHIMOTO
yumi-yoshimoto.com
@yumi__yoshimoto
@keshiki_designby_yumiyoshimoto

Holli Zollinger
hollizollinger.com
@hollizollinger

front cover: (outside to inside): Heather Moore, Ink & Spindle, Giuseppe Ribaudo
back cover: top: © Amorfo Photography, bottom left: courtesy Sally Kelly, bottom right: © Rajshekhar Kundu
5: © Abby Gilchrist
8: (clockwise from top left) © Abby Gilchrist; courtesy Ruby Star Society; courtesy Ink & Spindle; © Liberty Fabric Ltd; © Esther Huynh; © Abby Gilchrist
10–11: © Destiny Seymour

Bari J. Ackerman
12, 14 top, 18 top and middle: courtesy Bari J. Ackerman
13 top, 18 middle, 18 bottom left: © Bari J. Ackerman
13 bottom, 14 bottom, 15, 16 both, 17, 18 bottom right, 19 both: © Art Gallery Fabrics

Stacie Bloomfield
20 left, 22 bottom, 23 bottom, 24, 25 bottom: © Nikki Toth
20 right, 21 bottom, 22 top, 26 top: © Molly Thrasher
21 top, 23 top, 25 top, 26 bottom, 27: courtesy Stacie Bloomfield

Pat Bravo
28–35 all: © Art Gallery Fabrics

Erin Dollar
36–38 all, 40 all, 43 bottom right: courtesy Erin Dollar
39 top: © Jessica Comingore
39 bottom, 43 bottom left: © Laure Joliet
41, 42, 43 top: © Abigail Grey

Kaffe Fassett
44: © Lily Piel Photography
45–47, 49 both, 50 right, 51, 52 bottom, 53, 54, 55 bottom: © Kaffe Fassett Studio
48, 50 left, 52 top, 55 top: © Abby Gilchrist

Erin Flett
56, 60–61, 62 all, 64, 65 top: © Erin Little
57, 59, 63 both, 65 bottom left and right: © Erin Flett

Alison Glass
66, 67 right, 68 top left, 70 top, 70 bottom left: © Alicia Bruce
67 left, 68 top right and bottom, 69, 71, 72 both, 73 top, 74, 75: courtesy Alison Glass
70 bottom right, 73 bottom: © Giuseppe Ribaudo

Jen Hewett
76–85 all: © Jen Hewett

Ink & Spindle
86: © Ink & Spindle
87 left, 88 both, 89, 90–91, 93, 94, 96 top, 97: © Amorfo Photography
87 right top and bottom, 92 both, 95 all, 96 bottom: © Ink & Spindle

Naomi Ito
98–109 all: courtesy Naomi Ito

Sally Kelly
110 left, 110 bottom right, 112 all, 120 top: courtesy Sally Kelly
110 top right, 111, 113, 114–15 all: © Liberty Fabric Ltd
116: © Sally Kelly
117 left and bottom, right, 120 bottom, 121 both: courtesy Sally Kelly and Windham Fabrics
117 top, right: © John Doughty Spy Photography
118: courtesy Highgrove Enterprises
119: © GAP Photos/Highgrove–A. Butler

Cecilia Mok
122 top, 127: © Christian Holmes
122 middle and bottom, 124 both, 126 top, 130 top, 131: courtesy Cecilia Mok
123, 125 both, 126 bottom, 128, 129 both, 130 bottom: © Abby Gilchrist

Heather Moore
132: © Damir K
133–43 all: courtesy Heather Moore

Giuseppe A. Ribaudo
44, 145 right, 146, 147 all, 148 right, 149, 150 bottom, 151 both: courtesy Giuseppe Ribaudo
145 left, 148 left: © Stephen Koharian
150 top: © Demetre Edwards

Katarina Dragutinović Roccella
152–59 all, 161: courtesy Katarina Roccella
160: © Art Gallery Fabrics

Ruby Star Society
162–71 all, 178–93 all: courtesy Ruby Star Society
172–77 all: courtesy Melody Miller and Ruby Star Society
194–95 all: courtesy Sarah Watts

Destiny Seymour
196: © Destiny Seymour
197 left, 200–201, 202, 203 top and bottom left, 207: © Alan Greyeyes
197 top and bottom right, 198 both, 199, 203 bottom right, 204, 205 all, 206: © Destiny Seymour

Mili Suleman
208, 209 left, 210 both, 213 right, 216 top left and right: © Esther Huynh
209 right, 211, 212 both, 214 top, 216 bottom, 219: courtesy Mili Suleman
213 left: © Marisa Vitale
214 bottom, 215, 218: © Rajshekhar Kundu
217: © Katie Nixon

Amy van Luijk
220, 221 left, 222 top, 225, 231 bottom: © Amy van Luijk
221 top right, 222 bottom, 224, 226–27, 228 both, 229: © Bonny Beattie
221 bottom right, 230, 231 top: © Abby Gilchrist
223 both: © Figo

Yumi Yoshimoto
232–43 all: courtesy Yumi Yoshimoto

Holli Zollinger
244 top, 246 top: © Lily Piel Photography
244 bottom, 247, 248 right: © Abby Gilchrist
245 both, 246 bottom, 248 left, 249, 250 both, 251: courtesy Holli Zollinger

252: courtesy Ruby Star Society